NIETZSCHE AND RACE

NIETZSCHE AND RACE

MARC DE LAUNAY

Translated by Sylvia Gorelick

THE UNIVERSITY OF CHICAGO PRESS

Chicago and London

The University of Chicago Press, Chicago 60637
The University of Chicago Press, Ltd., London
© 2023 by The University of Chicago
All rights reserved. No part of this book may be used or reproduced in any
manner whatsoever without written permission, except in the case of brief
quotations in critical articles and reviews. For more information, contact the
University of Chicago Press, 1427 E. 60th St., Chicago, IL 60637.
Published 2023
Printed in the United States of America

32 31 30 29 28 27 26 25 24 23   1 2 3 4 5

ISBN-13: 978-0-226-81972-3 (cloth)
ISBN-13: 978-0-226-81973-0 (e-book)
DOI: https://doi.org/10.7208/chicago/9780226819730.001.0001

Originally published in French as *Nietzsche et la race* © Éditions du Seuil, 2020.
Collection *La Librairie du XXIe siècle*, sous la direction de Maurice Olender.

Library of Congress Cataloging-in-Publication Data
Names: Launay, Marc B. de, author. | Gorelick, Sylvia, translator.
Title: Nietzsche and race / Marc de Launay ; translated by Sylvia Gorelick.
Other titles: Nietzsche et la race. English
Description: Chicago : The University of Chicago Press, 2023. | Includes
  bibliographical references and index.
Identifiers: LCCN 2022042408 | ISBN 9780226819723 (cloth) | ISBN
  9780226819730 (ebook)
Subjects: LCSH: Nietzsche, Friedrich Wilhelm, 1844–1900—Influence. |
  National socialism and philosophy. | Racism.
Classification: LCC B3317 .L277813 2023 | DDC 193—dc23/eng/20221021
LC record available at https://lccn.loc.gov/2022042408

♾ This paper meets the requirements of ANSI/NISO Z39.48-1992
(Permanence of Paper).

Contents

Introduction

> I shudder to think of all those who will claim allegiance
> to my authority.
> —Nietzsche (letter to his sister, mid-June 1884)

Adorno wrote a letter to Thomas Mann on August 1, 1950, in which he told him about a book on Nietzsche he was planning to write in collaboration with Hans-Georg Gadamer and Max Horkheimer "to correct the nonsensical situation that Nietzsche is widely regarded abroad [in the United States] as the ancestral father of fascism, while over here they prefer to trivialize him into a kind of Jaspers figure."[1] The origin of the book project was a radio interview that took place the day before Adorno wrote this letter, on July 31, 1950, at the Hesse radio studios.[2] In this interview, Adorno pursues the goal he outlines in the letter, namely, "to distance Nietzsche from at least some of the caricatures that suffocate his thought today in public opinion." For, he asserts, the Nazis had "confiscated" Nietzsche, distorting him into "the champion of the blond beast and of German imperialism."[3] To counter these reductive and appropriative caricatures, Adorno, Horkheimer, and Gadamer, each in his own way, attempted to correct the false interpretations that plague Nietzsche's reception. The founders of "critical theory" sought to reconcile what they saw as his "ultraconservativism" with the spirit of "rebellion" in the name of a postulated affinity between these two tendencies.[4] Gadamer, on the other hand, leaned toward demonstrating that the tragic pathos underpinning the doctrine of the eternal return clearly distinguishes Nietzsche from a "social reformer." Adorno, meanwhile, insisted on and maintained the view of Nietzsche as a "man of the Enlightenment" while underlining the fact that "Nietzsche's hatred for traditional philosophy was in fact [. . .] the hatred of ontology."[5] But Adorno concludes this portion of his remarks by defining Nietzsche's relevance to postwar Germany as follows: "We must understand the very content of truth as that which is fleeting, ephemeral, and not what is eternal and lasting."[6]

The contradiction is evident, for no "man of the Enlightenment" could claim that reason is ephemeral and espouse such a rigorous historicism. What is more, Adorno claims that Nietzsche's reconstruction of *amor fati* as a consequence of the eternal return is a mere result of his confinement within bourgeois society. Gadamer has the last word: he attributes to Nietzsche the quotation that he "was dynamite," which was in fact a formula coined by a Swiss journalist in a review of *Beyond Good and Evil*. Of course, Nietzsche was charmed by the phrase and later repeated it. But it is striking that this conversation between these three philosophers, with the express goal of saving Nietzsche from doxa and ideology, closes with an evocation of Nietzsche's grave next to that of his parents in a little village in Saxony put into relation with the fact that he once said "I am dynamite," without "being entirely wrong." Saving Nietzsche thus consisted in briefly recalling that he shared Dostoyevsky's views (though not on Panslavism!) to the degree that Dostoyevsky seemed close to Freud; Horkheimer insists on the idea that Nietzsche, as a precursor to Freud, should be thought of as close to another "great psychologist," namely, the Marquis de Sade . . . Gadamer is the only one to bring up an essential point regarding the Nazis' reception of Nietzsche: the exclusive reduction of Nietzsche's thought to the "will to power" by Alfred Bäumler.[7] But Gadamer does not venture either to explain what this doctrine is or to look further into how the Nazis believed they could use Nietzsche; for Bäumler was an academic, certainly won over by Nazi ideology, but importantly, he was *only* an intellectual. While he was indeed a pawn of totalitarian power, he was not an ideologue with a position in the party.

Clearly, the rescue mission remains close to the shore and does not venture into the high seas where the threat of stronger waves would call for more robust equipment. In his text *Nietzsche—die Antipode*, Gadamer attempts to account for what he sees as the provocative nature of Nietzsche's thought "for a thinker of our time." He gives three reasons for this: the first is that Nietzsche considers himself an "experimenter" and thus introduces a radicality into his philosophy that makes it more difficult to "integrate [. . .] into the continuity of tradition." Needless to say, it is problematic to suggest that Democritus, Heraclitus, Plato, Descartes, and Kant did not have a comparable status. The second reason is that Nietzsche is a "deliberate parodist" and thus has "recourse to allusion to contort the meaning of the original text." This astute assessment, however, is not developed further, and goes without any reference to the long tradition of irony. We are thus left to conclude that, as is often the case in Nietzsche's reception, his interpreters have difficulty situating his irony contextually. Nietzsche's irony goes hand in hand with a deliberately exoteric use of the esoteric/exoteric binary, which is presumed to have a selective function directed toward his readers while at the same time being in direct continuity with an explicit form of elitism. The third reason is the excessive tribute paid to the "brilliant psychologist." But the argument for this is that, through his art of using masks, Nietzsche "teaches us to interpret the surface [. . .] as a mask." Triviality accordingly verges on misinterpretation.

These reasons in no way help us to understand why Nietzsche became the object of obsession and appropriation that he was for the Nazis. Nor do they clarify whether this obsession was inseparable from the question of race, which remains strangely absent from the rescue attempt as well as from Gadamer's semi-autobiographical explanation of the way in which he himself received Nietzsche. When he first addresses Bäumler's reception of Nietzsche's thought,[8] Gadamer pertinently indicates that it is wrong to place exclusive emphasis on the doctrine of the "will to power" without connecting it to that of the eternal return—and he gives Heidegger full credit for the recognition of this connection. This is true, of course, but Gadamer, like Heidegger, forgets that *amor fati*, the result of the "will to power" coupled with the eternal return, calls for a second articulation. Namely, that of the two first doctrines on the theory of a "conversion of values."[9] Moreover, and this is the essential point, neither Heidegger nor Gadamer takes into account the fact that Nietzsche explicitly stated that he intended to take "the body as a guide."[10] Indeed, the "body" remains absent from all the previously mentioned approaches, although it is a primary material basis for racial thought.

If the idea of a "rescue mission" is to be successful, it must not only address the question of the body as Nietzsche poses it, but also examine the relation that this thinking of the body might have with the racist core of Nazi ideology.

However, the very undertaking of the rescue mission remains problematic: it too closely resembles the attempt to correct the past rather than the effort to reestablish it, whatever the consequences. The "reception" of a work is indeed a part of its history, but it can't be given the privileged position of being a part of the work itself, even if it takes the form of a necessary prolongation. It should be an accepted fact that texts can be events of and in history. And although we are always dealing only with interpretations, it would be wrong to fall into a futile relativism holding the meanings of these texts to be "infinite" or "inexhaustible."

The difficulty lies not in establishing the objectivity of the effects produced by a work, but in demonstrating the relationship between an interpretation based on verifiable hypotheses and the ways in which its aspects have been understood, used, distorted, and even knowingly convoluted. Interpretations can only be as thorough as the analysis of textual phenomena allows—neither more nor less than scientific hypotheses on natural phenomena. It would be both naïve and irrational to deny the historicity that marks all interpretation—even if it does not essentially determine the interpretive act. Of course, traditions can have coherence and can be very well grounded; but they themselves are interested parties within a history. Every moment of reception and interpretation remains inevitably blind to the facts that it cannot discuss, precisely because of the effect of concealment that they provoke. No one can escape their own time, but so-called great works, and rightly so-called, have a re-markable capacity to anticipate—although we must be careful not to predict the past according to our current interests. Yet anticipation has nothing to do with divination.

When Schlegel calls historians "prophets of the past," he does not give them the status of clairvoyants but one that is closer to the original meaning of the word—namely, to be a spokesperson, no longer for the Pythia, but simply for the *res gestae humanorum*. As Vico puts it, *verum factum esse*, not in the sense that truth falls under the category of artifice, but rather in the sense that it had to be constructed, or perhaps, "reconstructed." Contrary to what we might think, this does not entail a debilitating form of historicism. Reception is not the criterion of a work's truth, but neither is the aesthetics of production that praises and honors creative mastery to such a degree that the work, in its self-sufficiency, is thought to have sprung forth spontaneously, without reflecting its ties to what it reconstructs through lineage and opposition. Under the latter lens, the author's authority is valued to such a degree that it is granted a supernatural capacity to escape history entirely. The difficulty is not, in such a case, to refute this brilliant authority, nor to attack the work by contest-ing the privilege that its prodigious creation seems to grant it, but to determine the distances it travels in relation to the context and tradi-tion from which it arises, to pay attention to its innovations and the intellectual logics that make them possible. It is even more difficult to show the historicity internal to the work, as well as the historicity of the terms it uses, works over, and transforms the accepted mean-ings of, or creates new meanings for. This approach does not follow a direct historicist path but engages a more delicate combination of constant reflexivity and attention to the fullness of a past moment. The meaning of works is no more reducible to what precedes them than it is exclusively generated by their posterity. Nor is it a pure revelation whose sole agent and custodian is the work itself.

"Rescuing" Nietzsche, therefore, cannot consist in "justifying" his positions that in retrospect are considered unacceptable by claiming that his more admissible positions compensate for them. Nor can it consist in advocating for a certain reception by disguising it as a form of divination. An example that comes up incessantly is that of the famous "blond beast."[11] The expression first appears in paragraph 11 of the first essay in *On the Genealogy of Morals*: "One cannot fail to see at the bottom of all these noble races the beast of prey, the splendid *blond beast* prowling about avidly in search of spoil and victory; this hidden core needs to erupt from time to time, the animal has to get out again and go back to the wilderness: the Roman, Arabian, Germanic, Japanese nobility, the Homeric heroes, the Scandinavian Vikings—they all shared this need."[12] In the same context, Nietzsche considers "blondness" to be a "Celtic" characteristic, but it is not, at the same time, the privilege of the dominant "race," since the phenomenon that calls for the noble "race" or caste to have its basis in brutality toward others—in contrast to the kindness, respect, and esteem accorded to peers—is considered to be general and to apply to all cultures.[13] When Nietzsche speaks about Aryans,[14] it's very likely that he's thinking of Indo-Europeans, but just as much of Dorians and Celts. In fact, the expression is criticized now due to an anachronism in cultural reception ("blond beast" was Heydrich's nickname) as well as to ignorance regarding the meaning that the term had in the historiography of Nietzsche's time. In that context, it designated the Byzantine emperor's guards around the eleventh century, most of whom were Varangians, that is, "Vikings" and Angles.[15]

We should be careful not to be too hasty in concluding that such terminology indicates a patent "racism" within the Nietzschean conception. Indeed, the second occurrence of the expression "blond beast," which takes place in the same passage of *On the Genealogy of Morals*, brings with it an immediate correction: "The deep and icy mistrust the German still arouses today whenever he gets into a position of power is an echo of that inextinguishable horror with which Europe observed for centuries that raging of the blond Germanic beast (although between the old Germanic tribes and us Germans there exists hardly a conceptual relationship, let alone one of blood)."[16] It is impossible to identify the Germanic beast with the young commanders of Guderian's tanks or with the figure of the Aryan Nazi as constructed—without, however, arriving at a single definition that was not solely negative—by the *Schwarze Korps* or the *Stürmer*. From the viewpoint of interpretive method, making Nietzsche both the precursor and the theoretician of Nazi Aryanism presupposes a kind of reversibility of conceptual organizations, discourses, and the "system" such that it relies on the erasure of the necessarily historical aspect of the object in question. In other words, it simultaneously presupposes that there is no history and that history exists in an entirely linear and predetermined form.

In a different context, that of the history of science, Georges Canguilhem takes up Koyré's warning, marked by a certain mischievousness: "The notion of a 'precursor' is a very dangerous one for the historian. [. . .] It is [. . .] obvious [. . .] that no-one has ever regarded himself as the 'precursor' of someone else, nor been able to do so."[17] At the same time, he draws on J. T. Clark's assertion that the "precursor virus"[18] should be eliminated when evaluating the practical effects of a theory. Canguilhem advances the following definition: "A precursor is a thinker, a researcher who, a long time ago, forged a path that has been completed more recently by someone else [. . .]. Before comparing two trajectories along the same path, it is important to make sure that it is in fact the same path. [. . .] A precursor is a thinker in multiple times—their own, and that of those who are designated as the followers and the executors of their unfinished work."[19] The use of the term "precursor" implies an identity of objects and modalities of thought without any distinction between the "logical time" of the establishment of claims considered to be true and the "historical time" of their conception. In the absence of this distinction, it is all too easy to apply a schema conjoining the anticipation and the fulfillment of an idea. From the viewpoint of the hermeneutics of texts, this has disastrous consequences. First of all, texts are reduced to the themes they are seen as expressing indifferently. Second, they are considered to be written not "against" a particular condition of the art they seek to modify, nor "for" an objective, impossible to see as an effective goal. Thus, they are not situated in any context that they can be understood as transforming and thus becoming a part of. Rather, they are viewed solely in terms of a unique path within one and only one cultural-historical development, whose concerns they reflect—concerns just as exterior to them as their themes. Finally, cultural history is not the chronicle of a thematic overview given in advance (when? by whom or by what?) that people might be able to grab hold of in order to actualize it progressively, and thus bring science or knowledge to its completion.

The distinction between "theme" and "style" rests on an incorrect conception of what a text is, whether the text in question is one of literature, philosophy, or theology. For it does not pay adequate attention to the fact that what an author says cannot be separated from the way in which they say it. And the "meaning" of what is said depends on the means of expression much more than on a theme determined in retrospect.

The Nazis did not need the way in which Nietzsche spoke of Aryanism in order to establish one of the essential axes of their genocidal project. What is even more striking is that this essential and essentialist notion was never given a rigorous definition in the Hitlerian context. In fact, the ideological and practical profit of the idea is inversely proportional to any definitional effort around it. This notion, which was not powerful enough to become a concept, could be weaponized at any moment as a slogan that suited the interests of the time as well as the context, since the mortmain of reflexive precision simply reinforced the party's stronghold of policing. To give one example among the hundreds and even thousands that exist, this is the way in which Bäumler, supposedly an expert in Nietzsche's thought,[20] installs his ideological conception of the place of Germany in cultural history: "What would Europe be without the Germanic North? What would Europe be without Germany? A Roman colony." The evocation of virtues considered to be proper to the Nordic "race" takes as its supposed basis a passage in which Nietzsche affirms his deep solidarity with the "Hyperboreans."[21] This people, referred to by Herodotus as somewhat spectacular,[22] are considered to live precisely *beyond* the North, as the very composition of their name in Greek indicates—Borea signifies the north wind. Pindar's verses are the obvious reference for Nietzsche, despite the common association of the "Hyperboreans" with Apollo, whose mother, Leto, was Hyperborean.[23] With this Pindar reference, Nietzsche emphasizes his "untimeliness" but, more important, clarifies the viewpoint from which he articulates his attack on Christianity: *beyond* the total decadence of an era dominated by "ancient tablets," in a place where no one has yet been pulled, destined, toward the "philosophers of the future" and "new tablets"—to the superhuman who *has not yet been born*, whose "reign" has yet to begin. Nothing here authorizes the reference to a Nordic "race," in whom Nietzsche could be seen to invest his faith in the future—though he places more hope in what he calls the new "barbarians," the Russians . . .[24]

In Bäumler's 1931 book *Nietzsche, der Philosoph und Politiker* (*Nietzsche, Philosopher and Politician*), the passage on Europe's debt to the Germanic North is placed in italics. Right beforehand, the author explains that Nietzsche does not have a "theory of the State" and that he was opposed to Bismarck as well as to his political plans, but that he "defined our task," which is "to be the guides of Europe."[25] The rhetorical mode of exposition that Bäumler adopts gives the illusion that his reference to Nietzsche is in full continuity with a commentary on what the philosopher actually wrote. It is very easy to recall what Nietzsche *actually wrote*—attacking the "sterility of nobility," a nobility considered to be the properly Germanic "racial" component, as well as "Germanic barbarism," emphasizing the lag of the (German) "North" behind the "South,"[26] thus incriminating Luther who would be one of the people responsible but, mostly, making a distinction between the geographic Europe and the cultural Europe. Nietzsche writes: "Here, where the concepts 'modern' and 'European' are almost equivalent, what is understood by Europe comprises much more territory than geographical Europe, the little peninsula of Asia: America, especially, belongs to it, insofar as it is the daughter-land of our culture. On the other hand, the cultural concept of 'Europe' does not include all of geographical Europe; it includes only those nations and ethnic minorities who possess a common past in Greece, Rome, Judaism, and Christianity."[27] It matters little what may be disputable—particularly today—within this hasty, only partially informed distribution of cultural components. For what becomes clear here above all is the pure and simple impossibility of finding within this the basis of a cultural genealogy that would justify any link between Nietzsche and Bäumler's ideological vision. The fact that Nietzsche's authority—if we can consider him to have authority on the fragile historical basis of these claims—could be summoned by Bäumler simply reveals the extent to which an ideologue will use tradition, or rather, abuse it, since, by virtue of their task, idealogues conform to the fantasy of the tabula rasa first and foremost.

Nietzsche's first use of the word "Aryan" can be found at the end of chapter 9 of *The Birth of Tragedy*, where it is used in opposition to the word "Semite" in the context of gendered accusations of sin. Nietzsche claims that such accusations apply to men in the case of "Aryans" and women in the case of "Semites." At the same time, the Aryan characteristic is the contemplative, Apollonian attitude, which, as we know, is overcome by the Dionysian with the power of a tidal wave. The "originary contradiction" that Nietzsche claims is at the heart of all things thus perpetually affects all "races." All aristocratic elites are called to witness the degeneration of the instincts that once guaranteed their exclusivity. Every subjugated barbarian will one day use the accumulated force of their *ressentiment* to conquer others. When Nietzsche speaks of the "Germanic beast" in section 11 of *On the Genealogy of Morals*, he immediately displays the light under which these questions are posed: it is the ancient problem of the "succession of cultural epochs," and the figure of Hesiod is summoned right away. In other words, Nietzsche's question is how cultures evolve and transform—that is, what is the "motor of history." Is this "race" in the sense that we now understand the term, or as taken up by "racist" opinions and ideologies? Nothing is less certain.

Nonetheless, the question remains and calls for an answer, especially in light of recent history, on the one hand owing to the erratic trajectory of the notion of "race" within at least the past two centuries, and, on the other hand, because of the fascist, and later Nazist, reception of Nietzsche.

Nietzsche under Nazism

A totalitarian regime rests not primarily on ideology but on rejections, dictated by social or political resentments (*ressentiments*), on aims, on the conquest of power, and on the perpetual struggle—both internal and external—of a particular group to maintain and extend that power. The representations necessary for this project of conquest include, primarily, negative or positive imitations of existing models that have been reinterpreted: namely, imperialism's many forms. It is only after this, to endow these representations with a certain coherence, and "legitimacy" if need be, that an ideology takes form. Often the very source of the ideology escapes it due to its complexity.[1] Such ideologies invariably include the mastering of historical temporality in order to replace it with an effective history, whether this be a fictitious one, an idea of "nature," the overcoming of nature, a history conceptualized through and through, or class struggle and the advent of communism, framed as the "end of prehistory." One of the consequences of this will to master temporality is the reconquest of a past that has been rewritten, remodeled, and, if possible, exploited to propagandistic ends. We can recall the anecdote about Goebbels and Fritz Lang that demonstrates the extent to which plasticity was a constant within Nazi ideology. Goebbels invited Fritz Lang to remain in Germany so that the Nazi Party could benefit from the filmmaker's fame. Lang objected, explaining that he was Jewish, to which Goebbels responded: "I'll decide who's Jewish!"[2] Fortunately, Lang did not place any trust in the master of propaganda, whose ambiguous invitations revealed to him not hospitality but the threatening possibility of changing his mind. Moreover, whether true or made up, the anecdote reveals precisely what was not contingent within this propagandistic situation. Reality is not the thing we struggle with by creating stories within the limits of what we know and can do in a given context, in terms of a recognized tradition. It is not what we react to, intervening in accordance with certain shared rules. Rather, it is *what we declare* it must be in terms of the current constellation of interests. Violence is thus instantly enacted, determined by the authority in place.

In other words, within a totalitarian regime, "ideas" play a particular role: they are never hypotheses that seek validation, but rather "expressions" of "reality as it is," its reflection, as enigmatic as such connections can be. On the one hand, "ideas" are understood here in terms of a double naivety: they *are* "reality as it is declared"—and the way in which this declaration is made is invisible or attributed to a foundational figure, identified with a dogmatic Pythia whose words various "prophets" translate. Since they have the same nature as reality, the ideas as such cannot be the object of debate: the political question comes down to the choice of one prophet or another, which is always subject to fluctuation. On the other hand, the "ideas" are applied *literally*, dangerously, since the primary effect of their "application" is the immediate mutilation of said reality. We must remember that no "theory" authorizes its own "application" without multiple forms of mediation, including technical ones.[3] The discredit cast on the technical, a consequence of the First World War, contributed in no small part to the undermining of consideration of these mediations in favor of frightening simplifications over the course of these declarations' application. The sphere of law, of course, was by no means an exception to this logic.[4]

On December 19, 1935, Carl Schmitt presided over the group of expert professors of higher education at the heart of the union of Nazi lawyers and demanded, in keeping with the spirit of the time, that the category of "man" be removed from the categories of law (*Frankfurter Zeitung*, December 19, 1935). Hans Blumenberg, who recounts this event, adds maliciously that "we already knew who the candidates for the category of 'subhuman' were, even though they hadn't yet been designated."[5] Indeed, renouncing a formal category of law was imperative in order to put in place a law that was *materially* founded on an ideology of "race" that distributed "humans" into different categories, that is "races" in a hierarchy designated as the motor of history. The "struggle between races" for vital space gave the notion an essential and substantial status. But, at the same time, belonging to a "race" was the new definition of the human condition, of "normality." That there were "inferior races" owing to their historical defeats as well as their insufficient capacities with regard to those of other "races" mattered little: they were agents of history, and if they had to disappear, they would have played their part.

Nazism was never Christian; the notion of a universal history of salvation was rejected. On the contrary, the affirmation of the hardness of existence, of the cruelty of historical life—these were the things the Nazi hero was meant to comfort himself with. In *Mein Kampf*, we can read, "Every historical event in the world is nothing more nor less than a manifestation of the instinct of racial self-preservation."[6] In other words, "the racial question is the key to world history." What we hesitate to call a racist "theory" or a "theory" of race, since the notions are so undefined and since this conception is so lacking in any consistency, plays a central role in *Mein Kampf*, determining decisions up until the last moments of Hitler's life.[7] It is founded on the notion that things are the same among humans and animals, and that interspecies reproduction is against nature, which in turn presupposes the aberrant idea that there are multiple species of humans that constitute different "races" ("Aryan"—which the Nazis were only ever able to give a negative definition of—, "Black," etc.). All forms of ethnic mixing are thus framed as suspect, and miscegenation is understood as one of the causes of the ruin and weakening of the "strongest race." Every species is fundamentally moved by an "instinct of self-preservation" that is "the primary cause that leads to the formation of human communities."[8] So each species having only a limited *Lebensraum*, while the self-preservation instinct and the instinct for perpetuation are boundless, the contra-diction that results is considered the true motor of history. Hitler writes that "nature" desires "the victory of the better and stronger and the subordination of the inferior and weaker."⁹ The same is con-sidered to be true within history, which is nothing more than the struggle to the death of peoples in order to maintain or increase their vital space.

Abandoning the legal category of "man" did not, however, echo the Nietzschean formula "We are weary of *man*,"¹⁰ but rather is a manifestation of nihilism to be framed in direct relation with the question that Nietzsche poses right before this formulation: "What today constitutes *our* antipathy to 'man'?—for we *suffer* from man, beyond doubt."¹¹

The Nietzsche Archives and the Reich

Thanks to David Marc Hoffmann's precise and rigorous work,[1] it is now possible to trace the evolution of the Nietzsche Archives during the period of Nazism and the Second World War. Elisabeth Förster-Nietzsche, Nietzsche's sister, who had founded the Archives (first in Naumburg in 1894, before they were transferred to Weimar in 1896) and begun the first edition of her brother's *Complete Works*,[2] was in search of funds, all the more so because Nietzsche's works would come into the public domain in 1930, in accordance with the laws of that time.[3] Nonetheless, no serious edition of his works could have been undertaken without the collaboration or consent of Elisabeth Förster-Nietzsche since she held the upper hand regarding her brother's manuscripts. Therefore, Nietzsche's sister would win in the trial against Kröner, who had to hand over the author's rights to her, while she was guaranteed the rights to the "Will to Power" manuscripts. She had so much power in this domain that she indirectly confessed to being the author of this largely unfinished book, and, moreover, Kröner would remain its owner and would continue to edit that version. The Kröner edition of Nietzsche's *Works* now includes Bäumler's extensive study—they omitted only the most overtly pro-Nazi passages and did not change the tone in the least. Moreover, at that time the Archives received funding from the SPD (Social Democratic Party) as well as the NSDAP (the future Nazi Party). Mussolini sent a 20,000-lire check to the Archives on what would have been Nietzsche's eighty-fifth birthday in 1931. A first publishing contract was drawn up with the Munich publishing house Beck, and the texts were prepared and established by a scientific committee including, notably, Oswald Spengler (until 1936),[4] Max Oehler, and later Martin Heidegger (from 1935 to 1942). Hans Joachim Mette and Karl Schlechta, among others, would also collaborate on this project. The edition was placed under the high patronage of the Deutsche Forschungsgemeinschaft, the chancellery of the Reich, and the minister of propaganda.[5]

At the same time, the publishing house Reclam took advantage of the works' entrance into the public domain by publishing an edition in four volumes, the first mostly containing a biography of Nietzsche by Karl Heckel, and the last including not a single work by Nietzsche but rather Alfred Bäumler's essay "Nietzsche, Philosopher and Politician." This edition was viciously criticized right away as it did not include *Human, All Too Human, Dawn,* or *The Gay Science.*[6] Simultaneously, a controversy arose surrounding the causes of Nietzsche's crisis in Turin in January 1889 which led to his convalescence and madness. Numerous hypotheses were advanced after Erich Podach's book came out, which is rigorously written, notes the lacunae in the medical documents of Nietzsche's internment, and does not fall back on groundless conjectures. It also takes Franz Overbeck's perspective into account—Overbeck was the only person who came to Turin to help Nietzsche and bring him back to Germany. Podach and Overbeck quickly became targets of attacks from Nietzsche's sister and her accomplices, as they took an unequivocal stance against the way in which Nietzsche's literary heritage had been claimed by the Nietzsche Archives. Walter Benjamin gives an account of this on March 18 in *Die literarische Welt.* He does not miss the chance to denounce Elisabeth for "abandoning Nietzsche to charlatanism." This is a reference to the photographs she had staged and had taken of her brother, collapsed on a couch and already deep in a state of stupor. Benjamin also emphasizes that "abysses separate [Nietzsche] from the spirit of ambition and philistinism that prevails in the Nietzsche Archives."[7] To shed some light on this charlatanism, as well as the deliberate falsification of the first edition of *Ecce Homo* (the documents showing this are included in the later edition published by Giorgio Colli and Mazzino Montinari in the French translation of the text), we can look to an example of the "corrections" imposed in the earliest editions of Nietzsche's unpublished fragments. Fragment 10 [31] from the autumn of 1887 reads: "The Revolution made Napoleon possible: this is its justification. For such a prize, one would have to wish for the anarchist collapse of our entire culture. Napoleon made nationalism possible: that is his limitation." In place of this text, the phrase on Napoleon was changed to: "Napoleon made nationalism possible; that is his justification." The passage was reproduced in Friedrich Würzbach's false edition of *The Will to Power* (§877). Nietzsche gives particular importance to Napoleon because he is, in his eyes, an example of the "superhuman" and "inhuman" phenomenon, like Cesare Borgia. The "superhuman" in question here goes back to the "superior man," which almost comes close to the "overman," but the "almost" here makes all the difference. The "overman" is merely *announced* by Zarathustra, but his time will not come until the end of the nihilist period, and on the condition that he succeed in understanding the Nietzschean prophet's teaching . . . To give another example of the coarse procedures to which Oehler had recourse, we need only point to the way in which he warps aphorism 251 of *Beyond Good and Evil* in which Nietzsche attacks the "anti-Jewish stupidity" and the "political ambition" which, precisely, are "symptoms" of this coarseness and bigotry.[8] In indirect discourse, Nietzsche puts these words in the mouth of these anti-Semites: "Admit no more Jews! And especially close the doors to the east (also to Austria)!"[9] In this case, Oehler has only to present these slogans as if they were Nietzsche's own words—and this is precisely what he does, without hesitation, in order to create the illusion that his cousin had put his philosophical authority behind Oehler's own ideological bombast. Like Benjamin and in the same journal as him, Erich Podach attacked Alfred Bäumler's edition, published by Kröner, without reserve. Subsequently, he was the first person to publish a serious study on Nietzsche's mental breakdown in January 1889,[10] as well as an investigation of the last eleven years of his life.

At the premier of Mussolini's drama *Campo di Maggio* (devoted

passed on propaganda that was completely indifferent to any scholarly interpretation of the work, as well as to the rigorous methods that it calls for. This explains the departure and defection of more cultivated and competent minds from the Archives such as Spengler and Heidegger, who, although they never took part in editorial work per se, quickly realized that they were risking their professional reputations by remaining in that environment. The interests at play at the Archives supported a tendency toward propaganda, in the enthusiasm of the first years of Nazism, without their realizing the degree to which the hazards of this propaganda and the fundamentally shifting nature of its goals and motives would push them not only toward deception but also toward leaving the scene.

There would ultimately be minds that were truly interested in transmitting Nietzsche's thought by means of genuine philological work. Schlechta can be seen as an exception during the Nazi period. Indeed, he was the only person to go to Basel during that time, in 1937, despite the hostility that had existed between the Archives and the university for several decades, owing to Elisabeth's desire to push Overbeck aside. The university's library held the archives of Bernoulli, Meta von Salis, and, of course, Overbeck. The Basel university archives and those of the high school, the Pädagogium, where Nietzsche had taught classes, held documents regarding Nietzsche, as well as Jacob Burckhardt's papers. Schlechta carried out this mission and officially informed the Society of Friends of the Nietzsche Archives (report of December 10, 1937). Schlechta was also the only one to remain, against all odds, faithful to the rigorous editorial project, even if his edition would be only an intermediary step. At the time, he was criticized by both Karl Löwith, who considered him overly concerned with philological details, and Erich Podach, who believed he wasn't concerned enough.

The "scientific" goal of the Nietzsche Archives consisted in publishing a work using the posthumous writings that would be as successful as *Thus Spoke Zarathustra*—a commercial success, of course, but also a cultural success that would have justified the efforts that, for a time, official propaganda was subsidizing and encouraging. This objective, that is, *The Will to Power*, seemed, to those who took part in its publication, to be Nietzsche's ultimate philosophical ambition.

The Will to Power
An Editorial Fiction

The theme of the "Will to Power" is prefigured in several
places in Nietzsche's work. These include *Dawn*, where
we find the expression "feeling of power" (*Machtgefühl*);
The Gay Science, where we see it appear in aphorisms 93,
113, 348, and 535, as well as aphorism 13, titled "On the
doctrine of the feeling of power";[1] and the chapter "On a
Thousand and One Goals"[2] in the first part of *Zarathustra*. But the first precise definition of the "will to power" is
given in the second part of *Zarathustra*, in the chapter "On
Self-Overcoming," a text written in 1883, the first version
of which appeared in an unpublished fragment of autumn
1882 (fragment 5 [1] 1),[3] where Nietzsche writes: "Will to
live? I have always found only will to power in its place."[4]
In the chapter "On Self-Overcoming," we read:

> Wherever I found the living, I found the will to power
> [. . .]. And this secret life itself spoke to me: "Behold,"
> it said, "I am that *which must always overcome itself.* [. . .]
> And even you, seeker of knowledge, are only a path and
> footstep of my will; indeed, my will to power follows also
> on the heels of your will to truth! [. . .] Only where life
> is, is there also will; but not will to life, instead—thus I
> teach you—will to power! Much is esteemed more highly

by life than life itself; yet out of esteeming itself speaks—the will to power!"[5]

We can thus say that this will is not a metaphysical principle like Schopenhauer's concept of the will, which "manifests" and "expresses itself" in various forms of life. The "will to power" is, on the contrary, another definition of life. Here, life is conceived as a permanent struggle between the strong and the weak, taking place within each of these two orientations of drives. But above all, "life," understood in this way, is a constant overcoming of the self, even if this takes place at the cost of life itself. The "will to power" is the motor that creators of values obey—values that they imposed upon themselves and that determine, for a time, what is good and what is bad. This "thesis" appears for the first time as the title of a book project that Nietzsche conceived at the end of the summer of 1885. But this project is no more unique than it is isolated. Indeed, Nietzsche developed many plans for many different projects, faithful as he was to the idea that the philosopher should be the "attempter of new possibilities" (fragment 35 [45], May–July 1885).[6] Other themes that Nietzsche was working on at the same time as the "will to power" include "great politics," the "good European," and the "tartuffery of the modern era."

If we consider the fact that many of Nietzsche's unpublished fragments play the role of a thought journal, where perpetual intellectual fermentation is the dominant process, we can see that it is already an abusive oversimplification to isolate a theme like the "will to power" out of the daily complexity of Nietzsche's intellectual process. In April–June 1885, in fragment 34 [247], he explains that "life" (that is, the "will to power") also controls the inorganic world, or rather that there is no inorganic world or would-be natural law, which means that what we see and experience everywhere around us are relations of force between masses of energy. This idea will be further developed in aphorism 36 of *Beyond Good and Evil*. Nietzsche thus extends the dominion of the "will to power" from the world of the living to the inorganic world, dissolving, in the same gesture, the boundaries that separate these two worlds. In May–July 1885, in fragment 35 [15], the organic functions are considered as "basic will[s]," differentiated according to the "will to power." This will is specialized into a "will to nourishment," a "will to possessions," for example, into a system of obedience, a system of domination that presides over the body.[7] The causality that Nietzsche believes in is that of will over will. But this causality is positioned in opposition to simply mechanistic causality. In the same period, in fragment 35 [68], Nietzsche characterizes the "will to power" in relation to the individual person. Although the individual is an illusion, although heredity insures a certain personal stability, the "will to power" moves across individuals because it needs "egoism" as a *temporary* condition of existence. But Nietzsche seems not to be satisfied by this formulation, which would appear to identify the "will to power" with a Schopenhauerian will, a fundamental will that manifests across a plurality of people, mediated by the principle of individuation. Instead, he attempts, for the first time, to locate the intuition of the will to power and that of the eternal return on the same level, as the title of fragment 35 [68], "On the Ring of Rings," indicates.[8] In fragment 38 [12] of June–July 1885,[9] unquestionably very important as it is the first version of the famous aphorism 36 of *Beyond Good and Evil*, Nietzsche again hesitates to place the "will to power" and the "eternal return" on the same level. He writes about the "ring of rings," a metaphor with enigmatic connotations, which refers back to the last book of *Zarathustra*, self-published in an edition of just over fifty copies. Not long after, in August of 1885, one of Nietzsche's journals begins with the title of a work indicated in fragment 39 [1]: "*The Will to Power*. Attempt at a New Interpretation of All Events."[10] Fragments 39 [12] and 39 [13], written in direct succession, enumerate the themes to be interpreted from the viewpoint of the "will to power." These include nourishment, reproduction, heredity, and the division of labor.[11] Some of these themes are present in the first two parts of *Beyond Good and Evil*: causes and facts, laws of nature, the refutation of a moral God, the will to truth—these ideas are all developed in the first two parts. The common thread here is thus the body, *Leib*, that is, the "body proper," the body of the person and not a "physical body" (*Körper*). But this "body" is nothing other than a "structure composed of many souls" (*Beyond Good and Evil*, <§> 19).[12] In fragment 39 [15] Nietzsche writes: "Now I bring a new interpretation [. . .]. Put popularly: God has been refuted, but not the devil.—"[13] This new interpretation is a prelude to fragment 40 [50] of August–September 1885, where he writes:

> Herewith under the not undangerous title "The Will to Power" a new philosophy or, spoken more clearly, *the attempt at a new interpretation of all events*, should have its say: as is fair only provisionally and as an attempt, only in preparation and questioningly, only "as prelude" to an earnestness for which initiated and chosen ears are required, as goes without saying, incidentally—or at least *should* go without saying—for everything that a phil[osopher] says *publicly*.[14]

Nietzsche refuses to use the "will to power" to affirm any definitive truth about the absolute foundation of reality. He does not identify the will to power with the essence of reality or with truth in the traditional sense of the term. In this fragment, we can find at once the idea that the "will to power" is an interpretative attempt, a prelude, and that in order to hear it, chosen and initiated subjects are required.

In fragment 40 [61], intelligence, will, and human sensations are said to depend on value judgments, and these judgments depend on what Nietzsche calls our drives—a common theme in his work at the time. These drives are reducible to the will to power: "the will to power is the last factum to which we are able to get down,"[15] that is, from the viewpoint of the structure of our consciousness, according to the perspective that we inhabit to consider the driving forces of human behaviors. But it is essential not to forget that Nietzsche never identifies the "will to power" with something that could be seen as a *substratum*, an "essence," in the traditional philosophical sense. Moreover, the expression *Wille zur Macht* maintains a certain ambiguity, for Nietzsche sometimes uses the term in the singular and sometimes in the plural. In fragment 40 [53] he specifies that he does not oppose reality and appearance but rather, appearance is the reality that is, precisely, called "will to power," designated thus because of its internal structure and not because of its imperceptible and protean nature.[16] This leads Nietzsche, more or less logically, to define the "will to power" not only as a fundamental desire, but also as a *plurality* of wills to power. We can see this very clearly in fragment 1 [58] of spring 1886, that is, during the time when Nietzsche was finishing *Beyond Good and Evil* and writing introductions to *The Birth of Tragedy*, *Human, All Too Human*, *Dawn*, and *The Gay Science*, and beginning part 5 of *The Gay Science*, as well as starting other project outlines, including one for a project titled "The Will to Power," which appears under a new title in spring 1886, in fragment 2 [73], "Attempt at a New World-Interpretation."[17] This falls among other projects, and Nietzsche lists the titles of ten new books that he's planning to write, including, of course *The Will to Power*. It is only in the summer of 1886 that Nietzsche gives a new title to this project, which he will maintain until August 1888. The years 1887 and 1888 were thus the two during which the "will to power" featured among his essential preoccupations in the form of a plan and book project. On the fourth page of the frontmatter to *On the Genealogy of Morals*, he announces this project as such. In fragment 2 [100] of autumn 1885–86, the title appears in this form: "*The Will to Power. Attempt at a Conversion of All Values*. In Four Books."[18] This is the first time we see the "will to power" associated with the idea of a conversion of values. The axiological question is here placed in the foreground, and the "conversion of all values" remains the subtitle of all later plans regarding the "Will to Power." In June–July 1885, in fragment 37 [8], Nietzsche redefines the conversion of all values as the supreme task of the free spirit. He had already introduced the expression "free spirit" in *Human, All Too Human*, and the second chapter of *Beyond Good and Evil* is dedicated to free spirits. In this period, Nietzsche names the great danger that he sees as a threat to the rise of life—namely, nihilism, that is, the tendency to risk depriving all existence of meaning. As he had outlined early on in the second *Untimely Meditation*, history and the scientific illusion inherited from the Enlightenment are primarily responsible for this tendency toward nihilism. Nietzsche's goal was then no longer to interpret all events, everything that happens, but to convert, to transform values through an opposition to nihilism. For according to nihilism, all values come down to a rejection of life. The following outline of the "will to power" project in four books is more or less consistent throughout all of his drafts:

First book: definition of nihilism. Second book: critique of morality. Third book: the will to power set in motion by the conversion of values. The contents and the title of the fourth book remain undetermined, but the "hammer" often appears as a metaphor for the doctrine of the eternal return's destructive power.[19]

From a rigorous chronological viewpoint, the idea of a book in four sections titled *The Will to Power: Conversion of All Values* dates from the publication of *Beyond Good and Evil* (1886), on the fourth page of the front matter, where Nietzsche announces his plan to publish this book. From summer 1886 to summer 1887, he was working on the republication of *The Birth of Tragedy* and *The Gay Science*. At the same time, he kept taking notes for "The Will to Power." A relatively long fragment (fragment 5 [71], dated June 10, 1887), devoted to nihilism, summarizes Nietzsche's thought during this period. In this fragment, it appears that Nietzsche wished to abandon the idea of the eternal return, concerned that it would still allow for nihilism. Then, he wrote *On the Genealogy of Morals* in several weeks. The critique of morality that he enacts in this book is clearly founded on the double origin of all values: we can see it again in the double explanation of morals that entails the division between what he calls "master morality" and "slave morality," a division necessitated by the "will to power." From autumn 1887 to February 1888, after the publication of *On the Genealogy of Morals*, Nietzsche was fully devoted to *The Will to Power*. The result of this work consists in three hundred and seventy-two numbered and ordered fragments. The first three hundred fragments have the roman numerals I through IV, indicating their distribution into the four books he had initially planned. On February 13, 1888, he wrote to Franz Overbeck: "I've finished the first version of my 'conversion of all values' essay." This is how he designated the "Will to Power" book project at that time. He continues: "In the end it was torture, and I don't yet have the strength to continue. In ten years, I will do it better." On February 26, 1888, he writes to Peter Gast: "You must not believe that I have written *literature*—this essay was *for myself*. Every winter now, I will write an essay *for myself*—the idea of publishing it is completely out of the question." We must take seriously this letter which clearly states that the work Nietzsche had done during

the winter—organizing these three hundred and seventy-two fragments on the "will to power"—was a personal project that was never
intended for publications but rather was a starting point. In the same
notebooks where Nietzsche was writing this outline, we can find
traces of his readings of Baudelaire, Tolstoy, Julius Wellhausen, the
Goncourt Brothers, Benjamin Constant, and, most prominently,
Dostoyevsky (*The Possessed* and *Notes from Underground*). At this
time the notion of decadence emerges as an important theme across
the quotations he takes from his readings, which include Paul Bour-
get's book *Essays on Contemporary Psychology*. This text gives a history
of pro-decadence movements, and Nietzsche was inspired by it. In
1888, he entered a period of intense literary activity, returning to his
preferred form of the aphorism after the three essays that make up
On the Genealogy of Morals. Between the spring and December of
1888, he wrote *The Case of Wagner*, *Twilight of the Idols*, *The Antichrist*,
Ecce Homo, and *Nietzsche Contra Wagner*. Simultaneously, his thinking around the "will to power" shifts bit by bit into a more general
context, evidenced, for example, by fragment 15 [20] of spring 1888,
where the "will to power" is no longer spoken of as a book in four
sections, but as a chapter among eight or twelve others. Here, he
writes: "The Will to Power: Conscious Becoming of Life." Chap-
ters 1, 2, and 3, meanwhile, are dedicated to the idea of decadence.
In Turin, Nietzsche organized the notes he had made from autumn
1887 to spring 1888 and continued this work through the summer.
On August 26, 1888, he wrote his last outline for *The Will to Power*,
in fragment 18 [17]. In this final outline, he gives priority to the axiological problem, but soon abandons this project in favor of another,
written in September 1888, in which the title *The Will to Power* is
nowhere to be found.[20] On September 21, Nietzsche returned to
Turin and finished *The Antichrist* in nine days. In the conclusion of
his foreword to *Twilight of the Idols*, he writes: "September 30, 1888,
on the day when the first book of the *Conversion of All Values* was
finished."[21] But September 30, 1888 was also the first day of year I in
the new calendar delineated at the close of *The Antichrist*.

Thus ends the project of "The Will to Power." Nietzsche never
fully treated it as such, nor did he work to bolster the initial hypothesis it was based on, developed in 1886. It is a fact that Nietzsche

had a book project titled "The Will to Power." He formulated this project in 1885 and 1886. He worked on it most during the winter of 1887–88 and ultimately abandoned it in August 1888. After that time, there was no longer an unfinished book called "The Will to Power" in Nietzsche's mind—therefore, it would be quite impossible to reconstitute such a book.[22] Yet the fact that there cannot be any serious justification for the existence of a book called "The Will to Power" does not mean that the theme of the "will to power" somehow miraculously disappeared from the horizon of Nietzsche's philosophical concerns. However, this overview of the unpublished fragments, plans, sketches, and outlines of the "will to power" allows us to see that this theme was located more and more closely in relation to the conversion of values. And if we need a conversion of values, this cannot take place without making significant links to an interpretation of the "will to power." The necessary rejection of an editorial fiction does not allow us to reject the philosophical examination of the "will to power" as a theme.

The "Will to Power"
A Concept

We must thus examine the idea of the "will to power" more specifically in Nietzsche's actual body of work. The first occurrence of this expression is relatively early, in fragment 23 [63] dating from the end of 1876–summer 1877—that is, during the period when he was writing *Human, All Too Human*: "Fear (negative) and will to power (positive) explain our strong regard for the opinions of people."[1] The last occurrence, as we said, is in fragment 18 [17], from August 1888. Is it possible to have an understanding of what the "will to power" is while taking into account only what Nietzsche published and wanted us to read? For the great majority of his published works, he proceeds in the same manner. First, he writes notes and drafts in his notebooks. He writes aphorisms, sometimes definitively, and then he composes his book through a process of assembly. That is, he chooses a certain number of fragments and aphorisms, at various stages of completion, from his many notes. Sometimes he reformulates fragments, sometimes he composes new ones. He then assembles this collection of materials into book form. Most of the time, he dictates his writings to a friend, starting from already written fragments and drafts, and these constitute the first manuscript properly speaking. Indeed, it is very rare that we have manuscripts written in Nietzsche's own hand from beginning to end. In view of this, as we will see, the "will to power" and the eternal return are exceptions. For the work that is generally preliminary to the book project on the "will to power" is, in this case, subsequent to the writing of most of what Nietzsche says about it in *Zarathustra* and in *Beyond Good and Evil*, with some additional mentions in *On the Genealogy of Morals*. Thus, starting at the moment when he has already completed the majority of his writings on the "will to power," Nietzsche starts working systematically on the concept of the "will to power" in his journals. On the subject of the eternal return, we have only fragments and very rare texts in published works, without any later work following the announcement of a book devoted to this idea, featured on the fourth page of the front matter to *On the Genealogy of Morals*. The work from 1888 on the "will to power" indeed functions as a kind of final statement, the outcome of earlier work. This indicates that Nietzsche's concern was more around finding a less allegorical means of exposition for this thought than that of *Zarathustra*, perhaps more developed than the one found in *Beyond Good and Evil*, and that it was no longer a question of clearing ground that had not been fully explored. The first text on the "will to power" appears in book 1 of *Zarathustra*.

What was Nietzsche's own perspective on *Zarathustra* and *Beyond Good and Evil*? We have a direct echo of it in *Ecce Homo*, that is, in the retrospective vision of his own trajectory. Yet the four occurrences of the expression "will to power" in *Ecce Homo* strangely concern neither *Zarathustra* nor *Beyond Good and Evil*. Even when the expression "will to power" is associated with the figure Zarathustra, in the preface to *Ecce Homo*, in paragraph 4, this is done only to signal that Zarathustra is not a prophet in the conventional sense, one of these "hybrids of sickness and will to power whom people call founders of religions."[2] The "will to power" here appears as a personal characteristic among other psychological traits. We realize this when we read the chapter "The Birth of Tragedy" in *Ecce Homo*, paragraph 4. Here, Nietzsche speaks of Wagner, comparing himself to him: "Even psychologically all decisive traits of my own nature are projected into Wagner's—the close proximity of the brightest and the most calamitous forces, the will to power as no man ever possessed it, the ruthless courage in matters of the spirit, the unlimited power to learn without damage to the will to act."[3] The "will to power" is then considered as a characteristic of Germany under Wilhelm II, that is, it is identified with the German Reich's appetite for conquest. This identification is found in paragraph 1 of the chapter "The Case of Wagner" in *Ecce Homo*. Finally, the "will to power" is cited in paragraph 4 of "Why I Am a Destiny," where Nietzsche places it on the same level as the desires and affects, recognizing it as one of the "terrible aspects of reality" within what Nietzsche calls the "great economy of the whole"—aspects that, he writes, "are to an incalculable degree more necessary than that form of petty happiness which people call 'goodness.'"[4] The "will to power" is thus placed in relation with the instincts responsible for the structure of the world, justifying Zarathustra's critique of "good people," of whom Nietzsche writes that they are responsible for "the most harmful harm."[5] In paragraph 1 of the chapter of *Ecce Homo* devoted to "Zarathustra," we read: "The fundamental conception of this work [is] the idea of the eternal return."[6] Nietzsche continues, writing: "My *gaya scienza* [. . .] offers the beginning of *Zarathustra*, and in the penultimate section of the fourth book the basic idea of *Zarathustra*."[7] This is the section, in aphorisms 341 and 342, where Nietzsche explains the idea of the eternal return for the first time, with the exception of aphorism 285. Also in the chapter on *Zarathustra* in *Ecce Homo*, Nietzsche writes that Zarathustra acts as the point of connection between poetic inspiration and revelation in the religious sense of the term. In paragraph 6 of the same chapter, Nietzsche adds that his notion of the god Dionysus is actualized here, that this is a revelation of truth, for Zarathustra thought the "most abysmal"[8] thought—this is how *abgründlich*, or "bottomless," is often translated, which also plays on the idea of an absence of foundation. We are thus given to understand that the most abysmal thought is not the will to power but the eternal return. Zarathustra is the very idea of Dionysus. In the chapter "On Redemption" of *Zarathustra* II, we read the following: "to convert all 'it was' into 'thus I willed it!'—only that would I call redemption!"[9] In paragraph 1 of the chapter "Beyond Good and Evil" in *Ecce Homo*, which logically follows the chapter "Thus Spoke Zarathustra," Nietzsche says that if he had achieved the "Yes-saying" part of his task by writing *Zarathustra*, he still had to execute the part of this task that meant saying No—that is, the conversion of values.[10] In paragraph 2 of this chapter, he defines *Beyond Good and Evil* as a critique of truth. He adds: "From this moment forward all my writings are fish hooks."[11] This presupposes that the majority of his thought had already been formulated and that it was now simply a question of disseminating this thought to carefully chosen minds, which is the mission attributed to the books written after *Zarathustra* and *Beyond Good and Evil* and, first of all, to the 1886 prefaces. In the following chapter of *Ecce Homo*, "Genealogy of Morals," he writes that the book consists of "Three decisive preliminary studies by a psychologist for a conversion of all values."[12] Thus, where we might have expected that Nietzsche would make the theme of the "will to power" the background of *Beyond Good and Evil* and *Zarathustra*, we find instead the problematic of the eternal return. The "will to power," as expressed in a scattered way in *Ecce Homo*, serves to designate phenomena spread across a broad range, where political ambition comes in contact with the personal ambitious temperament, but certainly not a philosophical definition of a fundamental reality.

And what of Nietzsche's letters? In his letter to Jacob Burckhardt of September 22, 1886, Nietzsche specifies that *Beyond Good and Evil* says the same thing as *Zarathustra* but differently. In his letter to Karl Knortz of June 21, 1888, Nietzsche writes: "Of my *Zarathustra*, I believe that it is about the most profound work that exists in the German language, also, linguistically, the most perfect. But to *empathize with* this will also require entire generations who first have to *gain* the inner experiences by virtue of which this work was able to develop. I would almost recommend to start with the latest works, which are also the most far-reaching and important (*Beyond Good and Evil* and *On the Genealogy of Morals*)."[13] In 1887, Georg Brandes had asked Nietzsche which of his works he should read to become familiar with his thought, and Nietzsche responded on December 2, 1887, writing:

I recommend that you read the new prefaces [of my previous works]—almost all of them have been republished. These prefaces, read in order, may perhaps shed some light upon me, provided that I am not *intrinsically* obscure (obscure in and for myself), like *obscurissimus obscurorum virorum* . . .—This could indeed be possible. [. . .] A philosophy like mine is like a grave—one no longer lives *with. Bene vixit qui bene latuit*—that is what's on Descartes's tombstone. A grave inscription, no doubt![14]

The link that he thus establishes between *Beyond Good and Evil* and *Zarathustra* is entirely justified by the very history of the preparatory fragments of the two books, which extend from summer 1882 to spring 1884. The drafts of *Zarathustra* are contemporary with the drafts of *Beyond Good and Evil* and the collections of aphorisms intended for the fourth part of *Beyond Good and Evil*. The preparatory notes for these two manuscripts thus stretch from 1882, right after the publication of *The Gay Science*, to 1884. Moreover, the 1886 prefaces to *The Birth of Tragedy, Human, All Too Human* I and II, *Dawn*, and *The Gay Science*, written right after the publication of *Beyond Good and Evil*, do not mention the "will to power." There is only one occurrence of the term, in the fifth part of *The Gay Science*, written at the end of 1886, in paragraph 349. Here, the "will to power" is defined as a "will to life" where the struggle for existence is only a preliminary restriction, which is simply a reformulation of what he had said in *Zarathustra. Ecce Homo* praises the sophistication and artful restraint of *Beyond Good and Evil*. This is a common theme of the 1886 prefaces, also present in the fifth part of *The Gay Science*, for example in paragraph 381: "One does not only wish to be understood when one writes; one wishes just as surely *not* to be understood."[15] This directly echoes aphorism 290 of *Beyond Good and Evil*. Nietzsche thus multiplies the warnings signaling at once that he is looking for companions among the free spirits and that these free spirits need to satisfy a certain number of conditions: first and foremost, the ability to read him correctly, that is, to cross the barriers put in place to discourage bad or too-hasty readers. In aphorism 27 of *Beyond Good and Evil*, Nietzsche writes: "I obviously do everything to be 'hard to understand' myself!"[16] and in aphorism 30: "Our highest insights must—and should—sound like follies and sometimes like crimes when they are heard without permission by those who are not predisposed and predestined for them."[17] For Nietzsche, this is precisely what distinguishes exoteric and esoteric discourse. While he explicitly makes this distinction here (*Beyond Good and Evil*, aphorism 30), it is rare that he does so in his published work; he does it a second time in *On the Genealogy of Morals* (essay 2, aphorism 27). But it can be found in a different form in a series of aphorisms including aphorisms 289, 290, 291, and 292 of *Beyond Good and Evil* (including the last aphorism in the book). Here, Nietzsche insists on the idea that every philosophy conceals another philosophy—that each word is a mask: "does one not write books precisely to conceal what one harbors?"[18] In the notebook of unpublished fragments that goes from summer 1886 to autumn 1887—the same period when he wrote the prefaces and the fifth part of *The Gay Science*—he laconically states: "*Exoteric—Esoteric*: (1) all is will against will; (2) there is no will at all. (1) causalism; (2) there is nothing like cause and effect."[19] In aphorism 56 of *Beyond Good and Evil*, the idea of the eternal return is present, even if he does not name it directly. Yet this abysmal thought is by no means the "will to power," since this last concept is formulated exoterically: Nietzsche always uses the expression directly, without making a mystery of it.

The difference in status between the eternal return and the "will to power" in Nietzsche's work more or less precisely reflects their respective importance, in the sense that the "will to power," because it is formulated exoterically, does not have the last esoteric word—rather, the latter concerns the eternal return. This does not mean that there is no link between the "will to power" and the eternal return. Rather, it means that the "will to power" is an expression that Nietzsche chose deliberately and in an exoteric manner, to communicate the eternal return to those who would be able to read him, to understand his "quarter-tones,"[20] indicating that this doctrine was essential to his thought. The link between the "will to power" and the eternal return is expressed explicitly in a fragment from the end of 1886, fragment 7 [54]: "To *imprint* the nature of being into becoming—that is the highest *will to power*. [. . .] The fact that *everything returns* is the most extreme *convergence of a world of becoming and that of being: height of contemplation*." The supreme "will to power," defined in *Beyond Good and Evil* as a synonym for philosophy, consists in embracing the eternal return. What is strange is that Nietzsche uses the expression "height of contemplation," since no contemplation in the traditional sense could take place any longer if being were completely dissolved into becoming. There would no longer be a need to contemplate even the smallest "idea," unless it were the absence or dissolution of ontology. The fact remains that the finality of the "will to power," its philosophical consequence, is indeed the eternal return. In a fragment from summer–autumn 1884, fragment 26 [325], Nietzsche planned to give *Beyond Good and Evil* not the subtitle "Prelude to a Philosophy of the Future" but "Prelude to a Philosophy of the Eternal Return." Which, without forcing any interpretation, means that the philosophy of the future *is* the philosophy of the eternal return, and that the last word of this philosophy, of what Nietzsche was preparing for by writing *Zarathustra* and *Beyond Good and Evil*, was the enigma of Dionysus, the enigmatic figure of the eternal return.

The "will to power" is thus a sign that should lead to the understanding of Dionysus's mask. It is a way of converting the notion of life and reestablishing Nietzsche's conception thereof. In this perspective, life is, in reality—once we've disposed of our own illusions and observed the effects of this—a conflictual energetics exemplified by the practice of artistic creation. What can we conclude from this position? We cannot think about the "will to power" without putting it into relation with the eternal return. The eternal return remains a kind of enigma that Nietzsche barely elucidates at all, since, once he speaks of it, it is necessarily in metaphorical form, illustrated by the reimagined figure of Dionysus. Indeed, the Dionysus of the mid-1880s no longer has much of anything to do with the figure in *The Birth of Tragedy*. Further, the "will to power" is identified with "life," but Nietzsche specifies that the final goal of life is not preservation, conservation, or the maintenance of existence. In the "will to power" there are as many ascending and creative forces as there are decadent and negating ones. If we project this conception onto the terrain of the "racial" debate, and supposing that Nietzsche understood "race" in the sense of raciology or in the sense that certain anthropologists gave this term,[21] the "corporeal" dispositions that are superficially observable are, like the "cultural" or mental backgrounds that are imposed on them, subject to "historical" fluctuations of "wills to power" in conflict. "Races" would be nothing other than transitory dispositions destined, of course, to enter into composition, collision, and competition all at once in order to potentially promote a "race" or "mixture" and to bring about degeneration or decomposition. The "will to power" is equally responsible for the conversion of triumphant values as it is for nihilism. It is at work just as much in the great health of the Greeks as in Christian decadence, in the (positive) emergence of the God of Israel as in the degeneration of this religion into a religion of priests. It is present in the figure of Socrates, who both results in Plato and embodies nihilism, the hatred of music and the belief in moral values as guaranteed by an ontology. The "will to power" is constantly identified with the idea of the conversion of values. It is, in a sense, the permanent motor of this conversion. A conversion of values is the result of a conflict between "wills to power."

Nietzsche analyzes the great conversion of values that has captivated the history of Europe for almost two centuries and that, he signals, gave rise to nihilism. This conversion of values is the one centrally set in motion by Saint Paul. Nietzsche then proposes another conversion of values—that of the Antichrist: "Have not all gods so far been such devils who have become holy and been rebaptized?"[22] It is necessary to put an end to the old conversion of values known as Christianity, which ruled for a time but ends in nihilistic decadence. A new conversion of values must be inaugurated, a new era of values in which, this time, the eternal return will serve as the guiding thought, and not the negation of life as in past conversions of values—particularly that of Saint Paul, as that is the one that we are still suffering from. Nietzsche's ambition is thus revealed: the philosophy of the eternal return marks the end of a naïve attitude toward the conversion of values within the history of the "will to power." Henceforth, it is possible to will a new scale of values *while remaining fully aware of the possibility of their decadent trajectory*: "Every virtue inclines toward stupidity; every stupidity, toward virtue. 'Stupid to the point of holiness,' they say in Russia; let us see to it that out of honesty we do not finally become saints and bores."[23] To affirm, on the one hand, that we cannot truly exit history, that we are necessarily immersed in it, and, on the other hand, that this history follows a constrained—though in no way teleological—course, is, in the same breath, to attempt to eliminate chance and prevent linear time from becoming an Ixion's wheel. In reality—that is, on the only level of "reality" we have access to, the level of appearance—history is a conflict of "wills to power" that reaches both illusory and temporary moments of balance. The most extreme point we can arrive at, Nietzsche says, in our interpretation of events, is to observe or intuit the fact that what happens results from permanent conflicts between "wills to power." This is precisely what philosophy had up until then neglected to acknowledge, refusing to take the body as the starting point and common guide. The body is only a temporary unity, in transitory equilibrium, which owes its relative stability and unity only to a certain balance of "wills to power" in conflict—a conflict of which it is the result. For Nietzsche, our drives are endowed with intelligence in the sense that they never cease to make decisions, to carry out valuations and appraisals of what they consider, egotistically, to be "good" or "bad" for them—that is, profitable for the economy of their release of force. They are thus moved by reactive motions, and these drives inevitably enter into conflict, superimpose themselves on one another, push us in one direction and then another, give us the illusion of our own personhood, of our own selves, of what we call our identity, our corporeal unity. But beneath this appearance of unity, stability, and balance there is in fact nothing but a permanent conflict between basic axiological movements. This is revealed in an exemplary manner—and this is the reason why Nietzsche devotes so much thought to it—in every process of creation, whether it be artistic creation or the creation of values in general, whether one is situated in science or politics. For what is important is that the creation process is both destructive and innovative, and that it is thus beyond good and evil.

To think what has never been thought before, to bring the unheard-of, the utterly new, into existence can take place only by drawing from the generative conflictual depths of a permanent conversion of received values. This perspective shows that one cannot rely on determinism, which is an illusion pure and simple, while all these illusions are necessary for the process of creation. And this is why it is always a contradiction to speak of the "will to power": there is no one "will to power," there is only "will to power."

When we put the different occurrences of the "will to power" in Nietzsche's published works in relation with one another, it might seem that Nietzsche himself is on the verge of succumbing to the intoxication of his intuition, to the temptation to believe that the "will to power" is the essence of the real. By writing that "the world is will to power and nothing else," he seems to be committing the same blunder he accuses the philosophers of: identifying an aspect of reality and hypostasizing it by making it into the being of all beings. In the second part of *Zarathustra*, the second appearance of the "will to power" is found in the chapter "On Self-Overcoming." Nietzsche follows a logical progression, no longer analyzing the effects of the "will to power" on the level of general history, but, within each people, the manner in which the "will to power" dictates individuals' attitudes toward values: "'Will to truth' you call that which drives you and makes you lustful, you wisest ones? Will to thinkability of all being, that's what *I* call your will! You first want to *make* all being thinkable, because you doubt, with proper suspicion, whether it is even thinkable. But for you it shall behave and bend! Thus your will wants it. It shall become smooth and subservient to the spirit, as its mirror and reflection. This is your entire will, you wisest ones, as a will to power; and even when you speak of good and evil and of valuations."[24] The wisest ones are not only philosophers but also those who create new values. From the level of the history of a people and its culture, we have moved to the level of those who have determined the evolution of culture in the historical-national context. Nietzsche always associates the "will to power" and the will to truth in the same way; that is, what is affirmed as a will to truth, the search for truth by the wisest, is, in reality, the expression of their "will to power," a nearly unconscious expression (to use a term that, in this case, is not an anachronism). We need only remember that the first chapter of *Beyond Good and Evil*, titled "On the Prejudices of Philosophers," ends, in aphorism 23, with the affirmation that a "psychology [of] the depths" is needed to examine these prejudices, and that this psychology of the depths must be joined by a "doctrine of the development of the will to power." He writes: "All psychology so far has got stuck in moral prejudices and fears; it has not dared to descend into the depths. To understand it as morphology and *the doctrine of the development of the will to power*, as I do—nobody has yet come close to doing this even in thought."[25] It is of course in *Beyond Good and Evil* that we find the most frequent occurrences of the term "will to power," in accordance with Nietzsche's idea of the role of this book; namely, to elucidate the doctrines of *Zarathustra* in order to find an echo of them among the "free spirits." The first appearance of the term "will to power" is in aphorism 9, also in the chapter titled "On the Prejudices of Philosophers." Here, Nietzsche refutes the Stoics' idea of a life lived in conformity with nature: "[Philosophy] always creates the world in its own image; it cannot do otherwise. Philosophy is this tyrannical drive itself, the most spiritual will to power, to the 'creation of the world,' to the *causa prima*."[26] This is a restatement, in other terms, of the second quotation in *Zarathustra* on the will to truth, as well as a specification regarding the identification of life with the "will to power." It is the "will to power" at work in Stoicism that transforms nature to make it conform to an ideal, that by means of which an expression of the "will to power" turns against itself, thus betraying the very fabric of life. For "life" is as much a product of nature as the tendency to oppose and struggle against life. This is the meaning of what Nietzsche writes in the chapter "On Self-Overcoming" in *Zarathustra* II: the "will to power" is the motor of a kind of sclerosis—not an ethical one but an intellectual one, in the form of not a tablet of values but instead a tablet of categories.

To fix a concept and consider that once one has access to it, one can master nature—this is the illusion that Nietzsche denounces. Indeed, what is the point of constructing in principle what one is, what one is destined to be? We can also understand why the notion of the overman, which Nietzsche clearly calls a metaphor, cannot be interpreted in the sense of just any conceptualization. A very clear passage in *Ecce Homo* alerts us to this:

> The word "overman," as the designation of a type of supreme achievement, as opposed to "modern" men, to "good" men, to Christians and other nihilists—a word that in the mouth of a Zarathustra, the annihilator of morality, becomes a very pensive word—has been

at every moment,"[33] all while admitting, not without malice, that this affirmation is an interpretation and nothing more. The motive behind this is a strong reaction against the link made by scientific positivists and the neo-Kantianism of the time between the laws of nature and morality. In that interpretation, the universality of physical laws would have universal equality as its ethical consequence; science and anarchist atheism would go hand in hand, and it is precisely in opposition to this that Nietzsche places "the tyrannically inconsiderate and relentless enforcement of claims of power."[34] We can now understand that the "philosophers of the future," the true philosophers, whose portrait Nietzsche sketches in paragraph 211 of *Beyond Good and Evil*, are those for whom the will to truth is indistinguishable from the "will to power": "Their 'knowing' is *creating*, their creating is a legislation [. . .]"[35]

It is in this way that Nietzsche describes the "overmen," those who know that the conversion of values is a result of the "will to power" and gives way to the eternal return. That is, it gives way, in advance, to the possibility of a decline of their own values. These overmen have no qualms about affirming their elitism, their "nobility," their superior irony.[36] The only virtue that these philosophers of the future possess is honesty: "Honesty, [. . .] let us work on it with all our malice and love [. . .]. Our honesty, we free spirits—let us see to it that it does not become our vanity, our finery and pomp, our limit, our stupidity. Every virtue inclines toward stupidity."[37] The four virtues that Nietzsche distinguishes as characteristics of free spirits are courage, sympathy, insight, and solitude—all synonyms for honesty and its consequences, which manifest in society as ironic courtesy, as he says in aphorism 284, outlining a self-portrait and a portrait of the philosopher of the future in the same gesture. But of course, the passage that remains the most explicit with regard to the "will to power" is aphorism 36. It is here that Nietzsche sums up everything that he has said in paragraphs 9, 13, 22, and 23, playing stylistically with quotation marks, the use of the conditional, and the provocative assertion that "The world viewed from inside, the world defined and determined according to its 'intelligible character'—it would be 'will to power' and nothing else."[38] This rhetorical game with quotation marks is intended only to underline the interpretive nature of what he calls his thesis—which is merely the affirmation of his own lucidity—and which does not seriously claim to have direct access to the world from the viewpoint of its intelligibility, since Nietzsche never ceases to deny the very possibility of such intelligibility and to attack both the Socratic doctrine and the Platonism of ideas. It is not possible, from a Nietzschean standpoint, to access the world viewed from the inside. Yet it is unavoidable to interpret this "text," and if we are honest, we must observe that our own cognitive apparatus is not only finite, limited, and sometimes unreliable, but incapable of evaluating its own capacities without succumbing to illusion. There is, therefore, no critique of pure reason. However, it is natural to form hypotheses on what the meaning of the "text" might be, and the hypothesis that there are a multiplicity of "wills to power" in conflict leads to the following general formula: "*all* efficient energy univocally [is]—*will to power.*"[39] We can thus understand that the idea of the "will to power" applies to the inorganic world as well as the organic world and, from there, that the "will to power" is identified not only with "life" but with all energetic dynamics. This is what constitutes the original contribution of paragraph 36. It is also the culminating point of Nietzsche's writings on this subject. Later—aside from the unpublished fragments of 1887–88 devoted to the book project—he will never be either as forthcoming or as explicit on this theme. The difficulty of this aphorism consists in Nietzsche's use of terms like "will" and "causality" that he knows are simply metaphors not appropriate to designate their referent, which is inaccessible to us. This is thus not a method in the traditional sense of the term but a "morality" of method, as we have a "duty" to follow an insight—that is, a "hypothesis"—to its conclusion. Here, Nietzsche advances the hypothesis of a causality of the will—although he does not at all believe in causality or the will. This hypothesis is formulated in such a way that what we observe as "effects" are understood as being dictated by a will—that is, by a discharge of energy, which commands our instinctive life. We can only access the world of our passions and drives, for, as Nietzsche says at the beginning of aphorism 36, "thinking is merely a relation of these drives to each other."[40] Furthermore, in contrast to what Freud says, the "will" does not act on matter—on nerves, for example. This means that there are no psychosomatic phenomena, and that the "will to power" must be understood as falling strictly within the realm of the intellectual. Using the body as a guide, as Nietzsche puts it, is thus not about positioning the body proper as a medium for drives that react in relation to it, but about considering it as a transitory state of equilibrium between energetic conflicts. And this is a reality of the same order "as our affect—as a more primitive form of the world of affects [. . .] a *pre-form* of life."[41] From this perspective, the only difference between the body and the drives is one not of nature but of developmental degree. Here, moreover, drives are understood as entirely "intelligent," entirely intellectualized.

The Overman

The events that Blumenberg evoked, namely, the decision of the Reich's lawyers to abandon the category of "man," undoubtedly have a certain relationship to the symptoms of nihilism that Nietzsche had defined fifty years earlier when he spoke of "*our* antipathy to 'man.'"[1] He saw the "weariness" that he identified as linked, on the one hand, to the "leveling" and "diminution" of "European man" and, on the other hand, to a process of exhaustion, and more precisely: "what is nihilism if it is not *that*?—We are weary of *man*."[2] Yet apart from this diagnosis of his time, which is woven into the exposition of his thought in the three essays that make up *On the Genealogy of Morals*, Nietzsche had thrown the idea of an "essence" of man into question two years earlier, in *Beyond Good and Evil* (1885). While this line of questioning presents similar dangers to those incurred by the later critique, it was motivated by different reasons: "There is among men as in every other animal species an excess of failures, of the sick, degenerating, infirm, who suffer necessarily; the successful cases are, among men too, always the exception—and in view of the fact that man is the *as yet undetermined animal*, the rare exception."[3] If man does not possess any characteristics that could be qualified as essential, his future makes way for a process of overcoming. As we read in *Zarathustra*, "human being is a bridge and not an end"—it must, indeed, "be overcome."[4] It is remarkable that the "overman" does not appear anywhere prior to this work, aside from Nietzsche's unpublished fragments and several occurrences in 1888, most pointedly in *Ecce Homo*. The overman represents a relatively late concept in the development of Nietzsche's thought. The undeniable popularity that this concept quickly garnered once *Zarathustra* began to be widely read, in the wake of the First World War, was, by all accounts, inversely proportional to its adequate comprehension. The convenient conflation of the overman with the "new man" promised by Nazism was facilitated by the fact that the few texts that speak of this figure remain laconic, and none of them offer a reasoned or developed argument.

The first appearance of the "overman" dates from the summer and autumn of 1882, just after the publication of *The Gay Science* and at the very beginning of Nietzsche's work on *Thus Spoke Zarathustra*: "The love for the overman is the antidote to compassion for humans: the latter would cause the very rapid downfall of humankind. A little more compassion among humans, and despair over life would knock at the door."[5] But directly afterward, this formulation takes a more poetic turn: "I love all these heavy drops, how they fall one by one from the dark cloud that conceals lightning within itself: the name for this lightning is the overman."[6] Gradually we can discern the emergence, not of what would truly be the "overman," but of the position that this figure will occupy in the process Nietzsche envisions as a whole. The arrival of the overman can come only after the "death of God." Moreover, this figure becomes a *telos* that is both personal—"I want to know so that the overman may live"[7]—and much more general, insofar as his arrival is directly linked to the scale of world history: "We create a posthumous justice for all of the dead and give their lives a meaning when we shape the overman out of *this* material and give all of the past a *goal*."[8]

The Gay Science opened with a long aphorism aimed at the destruction of irrepressible faith in the end of existence and history. Here, however, Nietzsche turns toward what he has refused up to this point: "What apes are to us, objects of painful *embarrassment*—so shall *we* be to the overman."[9] The overman becomes a kind of exit from nihilism: "hasn't there always been a desire to journey into the beyond or into nothingness or to become one with God!? All these colorful phrases served to express how tired humans were *of themselves—not of their suffering*, but rather of their usual ways of feeling."[10] As the prologue of *Zarathustra* repeats multiple times, the overman is "the meaning of the earth,"[11] "Mankind is a rope fastened between animal and overman,"[12] "I love the one who [. . .] wants his going under [. . .] so that one day the overman may live"[13]—this formula seems to indicate a necessary link between nihilism and a horizon of salvation, a new "era" in the history of "values" and even the coming of a future "conversion." This final significance is indicated by the end of aphorism 24 of the second essay of *On the Genealogy of Morals*, in terms entirely borrowed from apocalyptic visions and written in an incantatory tone: "This man of the future, who will redeem us not only from the hitherto reigning ideal [of asceticism and Christianity] but also from *that which was bound to grow out of it*, the great nausea, the will to nothingness, nihilism; this bell-stroke of noon and of the great decision that liberates the will again and restores its goal to the earth and his hope to man; this Antichrist and antinihilist; this victor over God and nothingness—*he must come one day.*—"[14]

This future mobilizes the "free spirits," whom Nietzsche sees as the true agents of history. He addresses these figures through his "prelude to a philosophy of the future"—that is, *Beyond Good and Evil*—and by casting what he calls "fish hooks." The short chapter in *Ecce Homo* "Beyond Good and Evil" begins with a fairly calm allusion to this situation: "From this moment forward [the years that would follow the publication of *Zarathustra*], all my writings are fish hooks: perhaps I know how to fish as well as anyone?—If nothing was caught, I am not to blame. *There were no fish.*"[15] The coming of the overman thus has a future "historical" condition: it is a phenomenon inscribed in a horizon of expectation and does not presuppose the existence of a people defined according to a nation or any particular political form. Nietzsche writes: "You lonely of today, you withdrawing ones, one day you shall be a people: from you who have chosen yourselves a chosen people shall grow—and from them the overman."[16] The new conversion of values thus presupposes an alliance among the "free spirits" who, having overcome the two previous millennia, will be able to bring forth new generations, instilling in them the "meaning of the earth" and "great health." It is only from these future generations that the overman can arise—this is what Nietzsche calls "great politics."[17] This hope, which takes the form of a prediction, is validated by the affirmation that "all that is great began as madness."

Yet the fact remains that the concept of the overman is problematic even from the perspective of Nietzschean thought: how can the superhuman be "the meaning of the earth"—that is, the one who will finally bring new values to the plane of radical immanence that would characterize the end of morality as we know it, and at the same time be a "hope," a goal suspended above history in its present form, which would take on the role of a regulatory end within it? Nihilism would be a "sign" that this history was in the process of shifting toward a new conversion—yet would the meaning of this sign be decipherable in advance? Could it be anticipated? If this were the case, then chance would have mysteriously vanished; in other words, world history would end by coinciding with an "essential history"—and Nietzsche would be this history's only prophet.[18] Nietzsche dismisses the question of finality with the following formula: "Humankind has no goal: it can even *set* a goal for itself—*not* for the end, *not* for *preserving* the species, but rather for *abolishing* it."[19] But this clearly amounts to a certain kind of sophistry, as the question remains unanswered on what basis humanity can "give itself" a goal that is not an end, but rather its own "abolition"—that is, the reflexive dimension implied by the expectation of humanity's transformation . . . of its own volition, through its abolition. This reveals a cosmic background that in no way entails a radicalization of immanence. Imagining the possibility of humanity's disappearance as a living species is by no means the same thing as anticipating its overcoming through the emergence of the "overman."

The consequences of perspectivism are well-known. This is not a matter of "natural laws," which cannot constitute what Nietzsche calls a "text." He writes: "Forgive me as an old philologist who cannot desist from the malice of putting his finger on bad modes of interpretation." Nor is it a matter of interpretations alone, it seems: "and you will be eager enough to make this objection?—well, so much the better."[20] Yet we read, just beforehand, that Nietzsche himself as an interpreter "might [. . .] end by asserting [. . .] about this world [. . .] that it has a 'necessary' and 'calculable' course, *not* because laws obtain in it, but because they are absolutely *lacking*, and every power draws its ultimate consequences at every moment."[21] However, the cycle of interpretations stops as soon as someone claims that "every power draws its ultimate consequences at every moment." Is this not simply another "law," a "law of nature," an interpretation that claims superiority over the laws of experts for the sole reason that it takes as its foundation a "text" that is considered more "authentic" than that of other interpretations? If, on the other hand, what Nietzsche calls a "text" is nothing other than what is accessible to us through "nature," then we return to the hypothesis that, behind the text, there is an X, indistinguishable from Kant's thing-in-itself. In this worldview, we have access only to phenomena, and taking account of this situation amounts to interpreting it. Furthermore, if such an interpretation takes the form of a law, we know very well that the scope of this law's validity will be subject to a development that will gradually modify its impact as well as its signification. But Kant, and particularly the transcendental critique of dogmatic reason, are precisely what Nietzsche rejects.

In other words, the overman has more to do with what suffering generates when the malady does not entail "symptom[s] of illness" but instead leads "to a *vision*."[22] The overman is indeed *to come* [*à venir*], and this future "vision" could well be nothing more than a whim of its creator—"often the son is merely the father's madness revealed."[23] Or, at least, the vision need not exceed the one who brought it to life: "Once people said God when they gazed upon distant seas; but now I have taught you to say: overman. God is a conjecture, but I want that your conjecturing not reach further than your creating will."[24] In any case, as multiple fragments attest, "[t]he antithesis of the *overman*" is indeed the "*last human*."[25] Nietzsche often repeats the idea that the overman has not yet emerged and, consequently, that even the "superior human," a combination of the nonhuman and the superhuman,[26] is not yet the overman. We should not be misled by the contemporaneous passage from aphorism 16 of the first essay of *On the Genealogy of Morals*, on Napoleon: "Like a last signpost to the *other* path, Napoleon appeared, the most isolated and late-born man there has ever been, and in him the problem of the *noble ideal as such* made flesh—one might well ponder *what* kind of problem it is: Napoleon, this synthesis of the *inhuman* and *superhuman*."[27] Even more unsettling are the rare passages— such as fragment 16 [85] from autumn 1883 and fragment 35 [73] of May–June 1885—in which the overman is compared to an Epicurean god.[28] Yet here it is less a matter of an identification than an indication of the position from which human ambitions, and the illusions that accompany and drive them, should be viewed.[29] This is confirmed by *Ecce Homo*, where Nietzsche reveals that the term "overman" was conceived "as the designation of a type of supreme achievement, as opposed to 'modern' men, to 'good' men, to Christians and other nihilists."[30] Reflecting on *Zarathustra* in *Ecce Homo*, he insists upon the separation of all that humans previously believed to be great and what the overman is meant to represent.[31] Likewise, in the chapter "Why I Am a Destiny," the overman is figured as precisely that which makes possible the comprehension of what Zarathustra wants: to conceive reality *as it is* and to become invested in that reality,[32] in full innocence and fusion with it.

Therefore, the overman is a projection of Nietzscheanism made manifest: the overman would be the new kind of individual for whom *amor fati* is entirely spontaneous.[33] We also learn that the overman is the starting point from which Zarathustra can teach the eternal return, for the overman is the one who will bring about this eternal return,[34] submitting the humans of the future to his discipline. While the overman thus represents a "transfiguration" of existence,[35] he is also called to "*return eternally*."[36] The last occurrence of the term "overman" is found in a fragment from the winter of 1887–88:

> Humanity does *not* represent a development toward the better or the stronger or the superior, in the sense that is currently understood. The European of the 19th century is, in terms of his value, far beneath the European of the Renaissance [. . .]. In another sense, there is continual *success* in individual cases within the most diverse places on earth and from the most different cultures where, in fact,

a superior type has appeared, which, in relation to the entirety of humanity, is a kind of "overman." Such fortunate cases of success have always been possible and always will be. And even entire tribes, generations, and peoples can bring such a *goal* into being . . .[37]

There is thus a kind of universalism of "geniuses"—in Nietzsche's sense of "free spirits"—which will never have need for "races" as a source of support or as a condition of possibility. The emergence of such geniuses, however, requires a structure of stark inequality: only a minority, born of free spirits, will have the capacity to take on *amor fati* and the eternal return, and to instate, in so doing, a new form of "legislation." Nietzsche views this legislation as a "formation" and discipline that are the antithesis of asceticism, an education whose principal goal consists in instilling the correct interpretation of the only "text" with which we are confronted: namely, the effects of the "will to power."[38] All the attempts to see in the "overman" an analogy with the ideological ambitions of Nazism come into contradiction with the fact that Nietzsche never envisions a "race" as the material support of special qualities. Rather, the "body" is formed by a discipline whose primary characteristic is that it is not shared by the masses. He writes: "Books for all the world are always foul-smelling books: the smell of small people clings to them. Where the people eat and drink, even where they venerate, it usually stinks."[39]

On October 22, 1883, during the process of writing *Thus Spoke Zarathustra*, Nietzsche sent a postcard to his friend Overbeck: "I am taking stock of *how little* I know Plato and—*the extent to which* Zarathustra Platonizes."[40] He could not have said it better, for if we must hear an echo with the "overman," it is to be found not in the aftermath of history but rather prior to it: the analogy of the "philosopher king"[41] is the only one appropriate to this figure. The one difference being that Nietzsche projects this figure into an unknown future, as he introduces the eternal return, henceforth taught by Zarathustra, as an eternal return not of the "same" but of the "similar" yet differing. Indeed, if the eternal return were taken literally, as the return of the identical, we would have to imagine that humans would be endowed with a radical responsibility with regard to all that they would do in the future, wishing it will always be so. This hypothesis would lead to an impasse: the overman would not distantly derive from the tragic hero who fulfills his destiny while knowing that his downfall is guaranteed and affirming that his cause is just despite everything; he would be a "theological" response to an empty heaven. Thus, he would become either a Christlike figure or a creative genius, ceaselessly innovating—in both cases, the choice would lead to the same impossibility: Christ does not return eternally, and geniuses remain rare, be they artists or philosophers.[42] At best, the overman would be nothing more than the result of chance, and it would be contradictory to call him forth with such pathos. Nietzsche's critique of Stoicism[43] substitutes the "will to power" for the cosmos: yet the overman can only be an emanation of this "nature"—and Nietzsche identifies philosophy with a "tyrannical drive [. . .], the most spiritual will to power," to such an extent that "what formerly happened with the Stoics still happens today, too, as soon as any philosophy begins to believe in itself."[44] But Nietzsche knew very well how to be ironic about his own assertions: "There is a point in every philosophy when the philosopher's 'conviction' appears on the stage—or to use the language of an ancient Mystery: *Adventavit asinus, / Pulcher et fortissimus.*"[45]

Darwinism?

The last occurrence of the term "overman," as we said, can be found in an unpublished fragment with the title "The Overman," which closes with this account: "Once it is possible to trace an isochronic line through history, the modern concept of progress will be neatly turned on its head—as well as the index by which it is measured, democratism."[1] As Nietzsche attacked anyone who accused him of being a "Darwinist," it is important to show how he himself approached this theory whose name, used in the expression "social Darwinism," might have seemed at one time applicable to his conception of a hierarchy of values while also referring to a configuration in which the supposed competition between "races" would take place.

In a fragment written in the summer of 1872 and the start of 1873, Nietzsche mentions Darwin very superficially: "Darwinism is also correct in terms of thinking about images: more powerful images consume lesser ones."[2] Another fragment from the same notebook confirms this early positive judgment:

The dreadful consequence of Darwinism, which, however, I believe to be true. All our veneration rests on qualities that we believe to be eternal: in terms of morality, art, religion, etc. With the instincts, we can take a step toward explaining expediency. For these instincts are already the products of a very long process. The will does not manifest *adequately*, as Schopenhauer says: it only seems this way if we begin with the most completed of forms.[3]

A bit later, in the summer of 1873, he speaks of Darwinism as a theory supporting the fact that what is capable of living amid infinite combinations of conditions of existence persists. Against Hartmann, whose teleology he critiques, he declares his preference for the Democritean doctrine of atoms and the Darwinism that allows for the appearance of "great individualities," even if chance might intervene to destroy them. In 1873, Nietzsche claims again that it requires courage to be a Darwinist, "that is, not Christian."[4]

We can observe that this first clumsy and uninformed approach aligns with Nietzsche's concerns of that time. He was then trying to construct a "historicism" bit by bit and seeking a foundation for his theory in the positive sciences, such as Boscovich's singular atomism, while at the same time attempting to distance himself from Schopenhauer.

But his opinions start to reverse beginning in the summer of 1875, when Nietzsche begins to recognize Darwinism as a "philosophy for butcher boys."[5] This remark shows us that Nietzsche was thinking of the beginning of *On the Origin of Species* (translated into German in 1860), which concerns the problem of "Variation under Domestication," that is, the field of raising animal species that are used for food economy (different species of livestock); well-known luxury species (canine species, for example); and those that are on the border between utility and entertainment (different types of horses). Beginning with the mostly empirical practices of breeders, and after his famous journey to the Galápagos, Darwin elaborates a theorization of these practices of selection, hybridization, and reproduction: "nature gives successive variations; man adds them up in certain directions useful to him. In this sense he may be said to make for himself useful breeds."[6] And this is what allows one to "possess and breed from the best individual animals."[7] Nietzsche seems, to some extent, to have accepted his confused reception of

Darwin until 1880, as this fragment evinces: "For humans it is nec-essary to experiment, just as it is for Darwin."[8] He borrows from this notion in order to claim that "We are experiments: let us also want to be such!"[9] He takes this idea up again twice in *The Gay Science* (aphorisms 319 and 324)[10] but then several times in different fragments ("Experimentation is the true character of our life and of every morality,"[11] "To make an experiment of one's life—therein lies the *freedom* of the spirit, which later became philosophy for me").[12] Evidently, it is never a question of experiments designed to produce highly performing individuals for the purpose of economic utility: "Our most instructive experiment, a vivisection of life itself . . . sim-ply over two millennia!"[13]

Nietzsche had begun to leave behind his early opinions on Darwin at the end of 1881,[14] assigning him a much more modest place: "These stolid Englishmen / With their mediocre comprehen-sion / You think this is 'philosophy'? / Putting Darwin on a par with Goethe / This means: *a crime against majesty—* / *majestatem Genii*! / First among all mediocre minds / —he is supposed to be a mas-ter, / and kneel before him!"[15] Thus, for Nietzsche Darwin remains an "aftereffect" of "Lamarck and Hegel," that is, an effect of a more fundamental historicism than the tradition of Plato, Leibniz, Kant, and to which Nietzsche himself claims allegiance "in matters of the spirit."[16] But starting at the end of 1886, Nietzsche's refutation of Darwin takes a decisive turn. A fragment from a notebook of win-ter 1886–87 (7 [25]) is titled "Contra Darwin" and poses several objections. These include critiques of what Nietzsche understands of his theory of evolution: first of all, it is not an organ's utility that accounts for its emergence (Nietzsche claims that it's the opposite); the length of time during which one property or another is formed does not guarantee the preservation of an individual any more than it is an advantage to that individual.[17] Indeed, that which benefits the "duration" of an individual may in fact be harmful to its strength, and what maintains and preserves the individual can also be an ob-stacle to its evolution, while the lack and alteration of properties prove to be useful as they can stimulate the growth of other organs. The individual is a site where several of its parts enter into conflict, such that its evolution is linked to the victory or predominance of certain parts at the end of this conflict. In Nietzsche's view, "Darwin overestimates external conditions to an absurd degree, for what is essential in the vital process is precisely the great internal power of structuring, creating forms and exploiting external conditions for gain."[18] Even these new forms, created out of internal processes, are not forged according to any goal. Lastly, if what is preserved is revealed to be useful in the long term, then it is a matter of "harmful, destructive capacities above all; the aberrant, the product of chance." In 1888, the matter is settled, and Darwin is not taken into account in the discussion of the consequences of the "will to power," that is, the "conversion of values" as a general theory of evolution: "Is there a type that will one day replace humanity? This is pure Darwinian ideology. As if any species had ever been replaced! What interests me is the problem of hierarchy within the human species, which I don't believe progresses on a global scale, the problem of hierarchy among human types that have always been there and will always be there."[19] Another fragment from a notebook of 1888 is the source of a text from *Twilight of the Idols* ("Raids of an Untimely Man," 14) titled "*Anti-Darwin*":

> As for the famous "struggle for life," for the time being it seems to me more asserted than proved. It happens, but as the exception; the overall aspect of life is *not* a state of need and hunger, but instead, wealth, bounty, even absurd squandering—where there is struggle, it is a struggle for *power* . . . One should not confuse Malthus with nature.—
>
> But supposing that there is such a struggle—and in fact, it does happen—its result is unfortunately the opposite of what Darwin's school wants, maybe the opposite of what one *might* want along with the Darwinians: for it occurs at the expense of the strong, the privileged, the happy exceptions. Species do *not* grow more perfect: the weak become the masters of the strong, again and again— because they are the great majority, and also *cleverer* . . . Darwin forgot intelligence [*Geist*] (that's English for you!), *the weak have more intelligence* . . . One has to need intelligence in order to get intelligence—one loses it if one no longer needs it. Anyone who has strength gets rid of intelligence ("Let it go!" they think today in

Germany, "the *Reich* will still be ours . . .)."[20] By intelligence, as you can see, I understand caution, patience, stealth, deception, great self-control, and all "mimicry" (a large part of so-called virtue belongs in the last category).[21]

Nietzsche used Darwin only in the first phase of development of his "historical critique" when he was looking for a fundamental basis for a radical historicism that targeted Christianity, that is, any providential thought justifying a morality by using "natural" data to support it. Nietzsche clearly sought to demystify the concept of "nature" beginning with *Human, All Too Human*, and particularly in 1880–81 when he developed his doctrine of the "will to power." In his book on the question of the "living," Canguilhem arrives at a formula that summarizes any enterprise that seeks to derive an ideological justification from a scientific study of life: "The thought of the living must take from the living the idea of the living."[22] This is exactly the programmatic injunction that Nietzsche wished to follow, except that the determination of that which is "living" took place, for him, outside any real scientific inquiry, regardless of his scholarly knowledge of the debates surrounding the reception of Darwin and the questions of evolution.[23] For Nietzsche, "life" and "will to power" are synonyms;[24] and "life" understood in the ordinary sense is immediately thrown into question: "Life is no argument. The conditions of life might include error."[25] There is no constantly ascending evolution of a certain species, any more than the individual represents a stable datum since it is the battleground between both "triumphant" and "decadent" drives, and the destructive forces that are also indirectly "creative" can, if necessary, triumph and precipitate the decline of one species or another.[26] Any idea of an "adaptation" or of a structuring conforming to a reasonable or useful goal is quite clearly evacuated here. A "species" (for Nietzsche, there have never been multiple human species) or what Darwin would call a specific "variety" is in no way a guarantee or a measure of long-term stability.[27] Even humanity, as we have said, may well disappear one day, despite the hopes placed in the coming of an "overman."

Eternal Return

The existing obstacles to understanding the eternal return are due in part to the ways in which it was long misread, and in part to the ways in which Nietzsche deliberately obscures access to it. Indeed, the aphoristic account he gives in many of his works inevitably leads the reader to become lost in a labyrinth of lightning flashes, stunned by the shine of each thought and unable to perceive any overall cohesion. If they do wish to piece together the full view, they are often more attentive to dissonances than to the general progression. Nietzsche alerts his readers to his methodology from the start of his philosophical work, after escaping the influence of Schopenhauer and Wagner, in an aphorism titled "Against the Shortsighted": "Do you think this work must be fragmentary because I give it to you (and have given it to you) in fragments?"[1] Yet Nietzsche's esotericism is singular insofar as it is explicitly announced as such, many times, and particularly following the publication of *Thus Spoke Zarathustra*, after 1885. While he was desperately in search of readers and even disciples,[2] Nietzsche's arrogance was such that he wanted to assemble a chosen circle, composed exclusively of those with an aural affinity with him, or who had "the most select ears."[3]

We must thus proceed with great caution when we approach the question of the "eternal return" and, so to speak, relearn how to read by trying to understand how Nietzsche wanted to be read. This doctrine indeed appears strange, and critiques rarely discuss it or, often, reproduce Nietzsche's own allegorical tendencies around it. Nietzsche himself admitted, in a fragment contemporary with the composition of *Zarathustra*, that "The teaching of the eternal return [was] the *turning point of history*."[4] When he speaks of it, he considers it "the most terrible thought,"[5] since its first consequence is "wasted humankind"; indeed, if there is no finality to existence, the latter is in vain. This terrible thought is also "the most abysmal"—Nietzsche says this in his last work, *Ecce Homo*, and in the first fragment to mention it, in the summer of 1881, this thought is understood from the start as "the greatest weight to carry."[6]

The only contemporary of Nietzsche's who bore witness to his thoughts on this doctrine and to whom he confided—an exception for Nietzsche, and even Peter Gast (Heinrich Köselitz) said nothing of it—was Lou Andreas-Salomé. She describes to us a slightly ridiculous Nietzsche, speaking suddenly in low tones and visibly in the grip of terror.[7] But perhaps we should exercise some circumspection when it comes to the testimony of a very young girl, which leads us to apply the juridical maxim: *testis unus, testis nullus*.[8]

The difficulty of reading, despite the obvious presence of Nietzsche's esotericism, is heightened in the case of the eternal return. Among all his published works, there is not one remotely explicit presentation of this doctrine. At times, he speaks of it without using the expression directly, as in *The Gay Science*, §341, and *Beyond Good and Evil*, §§43 and 56. Otherwise, as in the case of *Zarathustra*,[9] the phrase is used in the text but only as a chant, a poem, an allegorical expression of the theory. Moreover, Nietzsche is silent on the subject in his letters, as well as in the prefaces written in 1886 for the republication of his works by Fritzsch, which he himself recommended as the best introduction to his work. We must recognize, on this point, that the phrase "will to power" does not appear there either. If we turn to the unpublished fragments, we find some materials, but never a detailed account, while the opposite is true of the "will to power." Moreover, he deliberately proposes several different versions of the expression itself: *Wiederkunft*, the idea of some-

Leben], in what is greatest as well as in what is smallest, to once again teach the eternal return of all things—to once again speak the word about the great earth of noon and human beings, to once again proclaim the overman to mankind."[16] But Nietzsche closes this passage in which Zarathustra's animals are the protagonists with the following landscape: "When the animals had spoken these words they fell silent and waited for Zarathustra to say something to them: but Zarathustra did not hear that they were silent. Instead he lay still, with eyes closed, like someone sleeping—even though he was not sleeping. Indeed, at this moment he was conversing with his soul. The snake and the eagle, however, finding him silent in this manner, honored the great stillness around him and cautiously slipped away."[17] Thus, it is not the prophet of the eternal return himself who has explained his doctrine; on the contrary, he is silent and does not even respond to the animals who have presented their understanding of his doctrine to him. Conferring with his soul, like the wanderer with his shadow, Zarathustra, like Nietzsche, insists on remaining silent on this essential question, the very core of his "prophecy." And when, in *Ecce Homo*, Nietzsche explains to us "why he is so wise," the way in which he speaks about the eternal return makes light of the exact conception presented in *The Gay Science* and in *Zarathustra's* "The Convalescent": "I confess that my deepest objection against the 'eternal return,' my truly *abyssal* thought, has always been my mother and sister."[18] These signs indicate that, unsurprisingly, Nietzsche did not intend to return to the Platonic conception of cosmology. First of all, his philosophical interests draw him to what he calls, in the first aphorism of *Human, All Too Human*, "historical philosophy"[19] and not to the antiquarian impulse to revive an ancient doctrine. Second, his reading in the field of physics, the theory of thermodynamics and that of the conservation of energy, does not suggest anything that would lead him to adopt an antique cosmology, and certainly not a Platonic one, since this idea rests solely on the notion of a return to the same, guaranteeing the permanence of ideas.

Three fragments from the autumn of 1881, written in the same notebook where Nietzsche recorded his first intuition of the eternal return, demonstrate the progression of this intuition. What Nietzsche calls the "world of forces" undergoes no qualitative change or immobility.[20] There is thus always the same quantum of energy at work in the universe, and no energetic configuration, no body, is ever in a state of "rest." Rest, stasis, and immobility are illusions, in the same way that "atomistic materialism" is a fiction.[21] Within this universe where the same quantity of energy persists, there is no law of evolution that would preside over a progressive organization or harmonization of original chaos.[22] Only phases of entropy and negentropy take place.[23] Finally:

> The quantity of all energy is *determined*, there is nothing "infinite" in it: let us beware of such conceptual excesses! [. . .] In such a situation, can there be two things that are exactly the same, for example, *two sheets of paper*? I doubt it: this would mean that they had an absolutely identical genesis and we would have to *concede that all the way back into the farthest eternity* something identical existed, despite all the transformations and creations of new properties—an impossible hypothesis![24]

The precise context in which the phrase "eternal return of the same" emerges is that of an essential theme which controls the conception of the "will to power" and which, additionally, allows Nietzsche to demonstrate how the eternal return centers on this concept. This is the theme of incorporation, that is, the way in which a knowledge, a set of ideas, literally metamorphoses bodies when it comes into contact with them, modifying the structure of drives that holds them together. The eternal return was first conceived as a "new center of gravity," and the "greatest weight" is formulated in this way: "An absolute excess of pleasure *must* be proven, otherwise we would be choosing our own destruction, taking humanity as a means to destroy humanity. Only this: we must both balance and counterbalance the past—ours and that of all humanity."[25]

The second interpretive path is the "historicist" one, in the sense that the doctrine of the eternal return is indirectly expressed through other terms that, evidently, do not seem to stem from the concept itself but all of which refer back to a certain conception of history: "Noon," *amor fati*, "Dionysiac" (no longer "Dionysian"), and the "conversion of values." In the chapter of *Twilight of the Idols* titled on the "will to power." On the fourth frontmatter page of *Zarathustra*, Nietzsche announces the titles of two works: *The Will to Power as a Conversion of Values* and *The Eternal Return: Sacred Dances and Songs*. Following this and up until 1886, the eternal return appears in many unpublished fragments as the title of a work devoted to time. Nietzsche makes many assertions about the eternal return: that it is a prophecy, that it is connected to the notion of "Noon," to the expression *Es ist Zeit!* (*it is time!*), to the duality of noon and eternity, and to the idea of a new *Aufklärung* (Enlightenment) where the eternal return is considered to be a "*hammer* in the hands of the *most powerful* humans."[34] The eternal return is also directly associated with the "overman," the only person who can withstand this doctrine that, at the same time, serves as the instrument he needs to teach others.[35] From 1887 to the end of August 1888, the eternal return appears in all the outlines for his work on the "will to power"; it constitutes a chapter or a "book" within the work.[36] Two fragments give us a more precise picture: fragment 5 [54] of autumn 1887, where the eternal return is viewed as a consequence of the physical theory of the conservation of energy, and fragment 14 [188] of spring 1888, where Nietzsche rejects the idea that becoming could have any finality, that it could constitute being or nothingness, since "the world is a great circulatory system of forces and force centers; it is an infinitely repeating game."

The eternal return is inseparable from the "will to power"; it is the consequence of this doctrine and rests on the same Nietzschean interpretations of the general economy of energy, but it is more particularly a doctrine of time and, thus, of history. Looking down into the abyss of the "most world-denying" thought—this is how Nietzsche described himself in his early Schopenhauerian, pessimistic period—may have "opened his eyes to the opposite ideal: the ideal of the most high-spirited, alive, and world-affirming human being who has not only come to terms and learned to get along with whatever was and is, but who wants to have *what was and is* repeated into all eternity, shouting insatiably *da capo*."[37] Aphorisms 56 of *Beyond Good and Evil* ends with the famous *circulus vitiosus deus*. Along with aphorism 43 of the work—"In the end it must be as it is and always has been: great things remain for the great, abysses for the profound, nuances and shudders for the refined, and, in brief, all that is rare for the rare"[38]—and the penultimate song of the fourth part of *Zarathustra*, these passages contain the first mentions of the eternal return without directly naming the concept. They must be taken all the more seriously as their formulation remains somewhat allegorical. These texts do not seek cosmological grounding or scientific carefulness, but seek to demonstrate the eternal return as a "prophecy."[39] In this regard, two fragments from 1887 are especially clarifying as they bear witness, for the first time, to the express articulation of the "will to power" and the eternal return from the perspective of a history of values: these are fragments 5 [70] and 5 [71], the latter dated June 10, 1887, and well-known for its analysis of "European nihilism." The "will to power" undergoes metamorphoses, which determine the history of values, or the movement from what *Zarathustra* calls "old tablets" to "new" ones. Within this history, the eternal return plays the role of the "hammer": philosophizing with a hammer consists, indeed, in bringing an end to the values that have grown decadent to give rise to new values and accord dominance to these values. The eternal return is allegorically framed as a hammer; from a historical viewpoint, it is a "*midpoint*."[40] This allows us to understand both Nietzsche's insistence on privileging the "great Noon" and his own interpretation of his own role in history: "He that is enlightened about [morality], is a *force majeure*, a destiny—he breaks the history of humanity in two. One lives before him, or one lives after him."[41] In other words, Nietzsche becomes, like Hegel and like Marx shortly before him, a prophet of the hour of justice. The particular pleasure of this position consists in "[*being*] *oneself* the eternal joy of becoming—that joy that also includes in itself the *joy of destruction*,"[42] as Nietzsche says in *Twilight of the Idols*, a work whose subtitle is, of course, "How to Philosophize with a Hammer." Directly before this passage, he definitively links the "will to power" and the eternal return within his system, using the following formulation for the first time to describe the way in which Dionysus's name should be understood: "saying yes to life even in its most strange and intractable problems, the will to life, celebrating its own inexhaustibility."[43] For Nietzsche, after 1880, life always and only means "will to power."[44] This "celebration" is a barely veiled translation of *amor fati*—willed, accepted, and welcomed with a laugh by the superhuman.[45]

From this perspective, the entirety of the past becomes necessary and must be accepted since Nietzsche promises a redemption without remainder. In his last moments of lucidity, in a notebook dating from December 1888 to the start of January 1889, he writes unambiguously: "Even Christianity is necessary."[46] The redemption of "all that is past" is "[the] new tablet I place above you!"[47] as Zarathustra says. Like all "revolutionary" spirits, in the Gnostic sense of the term,[48] Nietzsche claims to bring about the hour of justice, which amounts to asserting a strange mastery over historical time, as he repeats the gestures of the French revolutionaries by instating a new calendar, a new era. This is precisely what he does on the final page of *The Antichrist*, where he pronounces that his "Law against Christianity" was "Given on the Day of Salvation, on the first day of the year one (30 September 1888, according to the false calculation of time)."[49] Indeed, Nietzsche clearly presents *The Antichrist* as the first book of his "conversion of values," the second being *Twilight of the Idols*.

The eternal return is the doctrine that allows for the theoretical complex of the "will to power" to become the motor of a philosophy of history, understood as a liberated history of nature whose tangible manifestation is the perpetual conversion of values. The overman is the one whose "most intimate nature" is *amor fati*. He faithfully awaits the hour of Noon that will bring about a genealogical critique and predict decadence, regardless of the system of values in place; thus nihilism is an inherent aspect of any value system. Nietzsche's position, beyond its mimesis of any spiritual redeemer, any false messiah, confronts head-on the major contradiction that troubles every philosophy of history: to master time, to be able to save the past by predicting the future, a fixed point is needed, removed from time altogether. This fixed point exists for Nietzsche, and, of course, it is carefully disguised under the mask of the great Noon, the motionless hour: "Toward noon, shadows are no more than the sharp, black edges at the feet of things, preparing to retreat silently, unnoticed, into their burrow, into their secret."[50]

If the eternal return were to be visually represented, it would be not as a circle but as a spiral—a figure without beginning or end, where configurations of values are repeated over and over. Not at every instant, in the manner of the nightmarish duplication of the identical within the "tables of values," destined to the same evolution of a thunderous explosion, stabilization, and decline. Just as the goal of the "will to power" is not the preservation of human life, the eternal return is not merely the return of our history of values. Rather, it more generally defines the historicity of energetic configurations that include our bodies, although Nietzsche refuses all distinctions between the organic world and the inorganic world.[51] The eternal return is the general law that accounts for the frequency of energetic flows. Superhuman life consists in living while knowing that existence has no exterior justification or goal, and yet taking part in the process that brings about decadence in the service of a new irruption: the control of bodies is that by which the superhuman prepares for a new configuration, while accepting its inevitable decline. We can thus understand how Nietzsche found his precursor in the figure of Spinoza, for he too subscribed to the idea of *deus sive natura* and to the idea that our only freedom is in knowing the causes that determine our lives. But through "Dionysus" the eternal return introduces a *circulus vitiosus deus*,[52] another conception of "nature"—that of an energetics that allows us to denounce all the veils of camouflage beneath which our only task is to recover "the terrible, basic text of *homo natura*."[53]

Peoples and Nations

"*To be a good German means to degermanize oneself*"[1]—this is the ironic and pithy formula Nietzsche chooses as the title of aphorism 323 of "Assorted Opinions and Maxims"; in German it reads, *Gut deutsch sein, heißt sich entdeutschen*.[2] This statement might mean not a prompt to flee Germany, drunk on a newfound and robust nationalism that goes hand in hand with a stunning victory over France accompanied by a triumphant unification process, but rather, from a more general perspective, traditionally understood as a critical leap, to go beyond the limits of a history of nations, toward cosmopolitanism. The only appearance of the term "Cosmopolis" in Nietzsche's work dates from autumn 1884, when Nietzsche was beginning to write *Beyond Good and Evil* and the fourth part of *Zarathustra*:

> "*Ô peuple des meilleurs Tartuffes*
> *Ich bleibe dir treu gewiß!*"
> —*Sprach's, und mit dem schnellsten Schiffe*
> *Fuhr er nach Cosmopolis*.[3]

Going to Cosmopolis is thus at once a gesture of flight, a reactive movement, and an act of tartuffery immediately contradicting the declaration of national fidelity. This is not the act of a free spirit but that of a hypocrite who supposedly wishes to be a better German without being a good European. Since the actions of free spirits are not reactive, any more than they are characterized by subscription to an idea of the century, the flight to Cosmopolis might suggest, as least, that it is better to adopt a universalist horizon than to enclose oneself romantically within the belief in a homeland-based cultural or political mission. It is possible that this quatrain is aimed at a certain Kantian, irenic, and cosmopolitical legacy. In any case, the one who flees for Cosmopolis closely resembles the "hybrid European"[4] whom Nietzsche rails against in part 7 of *Beyond Good and Evil*, titled "Our Virtues," where we witness a play of personal pronouns: "We immoralists,"[5] "you modern Europeans,"[6] "we modern men, like semi-barbarians."[7] This is also the case of part 6, "We Scholars." For Nietzsche pursues the exposition of his "Prelude to a Philosophy of the Future" by sometimes speaking from the position of free spirits, to whom this philosophy is addressed, and whom he can speak to with the pronoun "we," and sometimes writing from the viewpoint demonstrating the need for this philosophy to come as well as the effective arrival of these free spirits. In the latter case, he groups himself with his contemporaries, making himself, along with them, the target of his attacks, opposing "We Europeans" of today to the "good Europeans" of the "day after tomorrow."[8] It is therefore no surprise that part 8 deals with the situation of "us Germans"[9] through the problematic of the relationship or opposition between people and homeland, but always within the frame fixed by the second book of *Beyond Good and Evil*, which opens, in part 5, aphorism 186, with the phrase: "The moral sentiment in Europe today is as refined, old, diverse, irritable, and subtle, as the 'science of morals' that accompanies it is still young, raw, clumsy, and butterfingered—an attractive contrast that occasionally even becomes visible and incarnate in the person of a moralist."[10]

This part of the book is titled "Natural History of Morals" and begins with a critique of Schopenhauer—that is, with a double critique of those unable to embody the provocative contrast between a refinement of moral sensibilities and the clumsy, awkward pretention to founding a morality. From this, we can deduce that Nietzsche is targeting the European sensibility, attacking it in the name of another contrast that is just as provocative, and doubtless even more stimulating. This is the opposition that the term *Naturgeschichte* represents, which becomes instantly polemical when applied to morality. The "history of nature" refers directly to the organology dear to the Romantics—that is, the idea that history is identical to the progressive manifestation of spirit, where nature merely constitutes a single step in this history (that of the unconscious) and remains of a piece with the totality as well as with each of the organisms that compose it. Further, Nietzsche confronts head-on the adherents of any natural morality, comparable to natural law. The entire composition of *Beyond Good and Evil* is directed toward a reinterpretation of the very meaning of "nature." Moreover, the choice of this term as a chapter title is consistent with a constant practice within Nietzsche's style: that of privileging the dimension of antinomy—here, the opposition between nature and history—to demonstrate the extent to which "concepts" are incapable of reconciling antagonistic forces. The "natural history of morals" is a double contradiction and a double illusion.

Let us reread aphorism 9 of *Beyond Good and Evil*, a text that denounces the Stoic belief system—namely, that of living in accordance with nature[11]—in favor of a dynamic prohibiting us from looking to nature for a reassuring, immovable cosmos, and, at the same time, demanding that we distance history and becoming from nature. This is the very dynamic that brought about the fall of Stoicism. Consequently, a city or a state founded on laws supposedly deduced from nature, from the cosmos, on laws that the cosmos itself is thought to obey, would be a clear antinomy. Cosmopolis is not the horizon of a soothing universality where conflicts are neutralized, since living consists of "estimating, preferring, being unjust, being limited, wanting to be different."[12] Furthermore, life is nothing other than the "will to power" whose "most spiritual" form is the tyrannical drive called philosophy. And just as "the Stoic [is] a *piece* of nature,"[13] the philosopher of cosmopolitanism would also be the victim of the tyranny he exercises, which is just as illusory as the beliefs of the Stoics. This tyranny seeks to exclude all conflict, all rivalry between peoples, with the belief that nature obeys the irenicism of an immovable and necessarily good cosmic order.

Beginning with the preface to *Beyond Good and Evil*, Nietzsche rejects any attempt to unbend "so tense a bow [that one] can [. . .]

shoot for the most distant goals."[14] He asserts that in Europe, the fight against Christianity ("Platonism for 'the people'") has given rise to "a magnificent tension of the spirit the like of which never yet existed on earth." Just as it is in Europe that "twice already attempts have been made in the grand style to unbend the bow," namely Jesuitism and the democratic philosophy of the Enlightenment, one of whose avatars, the press, attempted to spare spirit from the tension of the bow.[15] Nietzsche also targets Novalis and his belief in the regeneration of Europe by means of the Jesuits and Christianity. In 1799, Novalis wrote:

> In Germany [. . .] the traces of a new world can already be demonstrated with total certainty. Germany is proceeding, at slow but sure pace, ahead of the other European countries. While the latter are occupied with war, speculation, and partisan spirit, the German is developing himself with all industry into a partaker in a higher epoch of culture, and this advance cannot fail to give him a great advantage over the others in the course of time. [. . .] A tremendous intimation of the creative will, of the boundlessness, of the infinite multiplicity, of the sacred particularity and universal capability of the inner man seems everywhere to be astir. Awakened from the morning dream of helpless childhood, a section of the race is exerting its first powers against serpents that entwine its cradle and seek to filch from it the use of its limbs. All these things are still only intimations, incoherent and raw, but to the historical eye they give evidence of a universal individuality, a new history, a new mankind, the sweetest embrace of a young and surprised Church and a loving God, and the fervent reception of a new Messiah within its thousand members.[16]

Yet Nietzsche attacks the cosmopolitanism of the Enlightenment on two counts. First, because it dreams of "unbending the bow," that is, it doesn't believe in the necessity of the tragic dimension of thought, of the presence of conflict in life. Second, because it shares the same presupposition as Christianity, that of "a disappeared universal piety."[17] This does not mean that any occurrence of the term "cosmopolitism"[18] in Nietzsche's work is absurd, as we realize in paragraph 2 of the chapter of *Ecce Homo* on *Human, All Too Human*, where he explains that the understanding of Wagner requires a refined intellectual cosmopolitanism. But here again, the term has a reactive connotation, for it is only in opposition to what Nietzsche calls the translation of Wagner into German surrounding the ceremonies at Bayreuth that the distance and space that go hand in hand with this cosmopolitanism are needed. At bottom, however, cosmopolitanism is equivalent to decadence, as aphorism 17 of *The Antichrist* attests. Once the Jews abandoned their triumphant belief in the God of Israel, by means of Paul, the kingdom of heaven transformed into a "ghetto-kingdom."[19]

The philosophy of the future and of the free spirits outlined in *Beyond Good and Evil* will betray itself without fail, perhaps fatally, once the virtue from which it must free itself becomes its vanity.[20] But it is not certain that Nietzsche remained faithful to this analysis—*invitus invitam demisit . . .*—in the self-praising paeans of *Ecce Homo*. This philosophy of the free spirits will betray itself as soon as the temptation to unbend the bow comes to light, even insidiously, and in particular, on the political plane. For beyond the will to peace, prosperity, and comfort, the danger threatening the tense bow is precisely the belief that one end of tension or the other should be privileged. Nietzsche does not present an alternative between "the man of prey" and "ordinary individuals" where the "Nietzschean" choice would be a Cesare Borgia type over a specimen from the Biedermeier period.[21] A similar decision is one of the dangers that threaten "a philosopher's development"[22]—if he wants to escape it, the only choice that remains is not that between branches of these kinds of alternatives, but that of the continual multiplication of alternatives, or "the burden and the duty of a hundred attempts"[23]—the maintenance of the bow's tension at all costs. This entails living an "unwise" life, a reckless life, permanently risking oneself in extravagant virtue, overflowing generosity, and seeking nothing in return. It is thus a question not of arriving at a contemplation of the play of tensions, but of working to reactivate them while standing at the heart of the tension driving every era. Nietzsche calls this the dangerous and "wicked game."[24]

Chapter 8, "Peoples and Fatherlands," is the penultimate part of *Beyond Good and Evil*. The book ends with the question "What is

Noble?" In other words, what is the "nature" of the free spirit? And, as is too often forgotten, the book closes with the poem "From High Mountains," originally titled "Nostalgia of the Hermit" in 1884, before its completion in 1886. The final ten lines of this "aftersong" present a cheerful joy in contrast with the initial, elegiac tone, mired in uncertainty. The poem clearly recalls *Zarathustra* and confirms that what Nietzsche aspires to—free spirits, signs of nobility, *Vornehmheit*, recipients of tragic and Dionysiac knowledge—is indeed about to emerge:

> *This* song is over—longing's dulcet cry
>   Died in my mouth:
> A wizard did it, friend in time of drought,
> The friend of noon—no, do not ask me who—
> At noon it was that one turned into two . . .
>
> Sure of our victory, we celebrate
>   The feast of feasts:
> Friend Zarathustra came, the guest of guests!
> The world now laughs, rent are the drapes of fright,
> The wedding is at hand of night and light . . .[25]

"Noble nature," which must replace "divine nature," does not celebrate her victory over the latter, but ensures that she indeed arrives "at noon," at the highest moment of tension between light and night. The victory that Nietzsche is so sure of is not the triumph of light over night, but the fact that "the wedding is at hand of night and light," and that "the world laughs." There is no laughter without tension, for it would not be "noble" to laugh at that which one has conquered.

As is well-known, *Beyond Good and Evil* closes, in aphorisms 295 and 296, with a call to the belief in Dionysus, figure of the eternal return, and with a kind of admonition of the reader, subtly addressed to Nietzsche himself, demanding that he position himself personally at the center of this tension, to escape the charm of what he has just written, as if to escape the temptation to take it too seriously. In short, it is a reminder not to forget, as Benjamin put it in his joyful formula, that "The work is the death mask of its conception."[26]

The fact that part 8 is not the end of the work perhaps suggests that political reflection cannot have the final word—nor, consequently, can it be a primary theme of the philosophy of the future.[27] The account of "Peoples and Fatherlands," which we expect to revolve around the theme of politics, opens and closes, strangely, in aphorisms 240 and 256, with discussions of Wagner's music. It begins with an analysis of the *Meistersinger* (master singers) and what can be deduced from these figures about German characteristics and temperaments and closes with the decline from *Siegfried* to *Parsifal*, which ultimately casts Wagner at the feet of Rome.

Just as "moralities are [. . .] merely a *sign language of the affects*,"[28] national temperaments have their own symbolic language in the music they produce. Thus "political" reflection is immediately enclosed by a cultural politics, that is, by the general economy of values. The geographical framework that emerges proves to be in no way national. Rather, it is that of Europe, from the Atlantic to Saint Petersburg and not without a pointed exclusion of England. Essentially, this is a Franco-German Europe in which Italy plays a key role. For Nietzsche the philologist and reader of Herodotus, Europe is by no means geographical. Rather, in accordance with one possible etymology of the term, it signifies a vast horizon, an open view of great distances.[29] Above all, it is a process of Europeanization, which itself, unsurprisingly, has a double orientation with a tension between the two. On the one hand, there is a downward Europeanization, toward deceptive and complacent uniformity.[30] On the other hand, the upward-moving unity of Europe is just as transitory; the "good Europeans" are a hoped-for future, but not the end of history, since history can have no end. To be at the heart of this tension means, in part, increasing the singularities of national temperaments by placing them in competition with each other. At the same time, it means sowing seeds for the overcoming of these singularities, such that this overcoming does not overflow toward the horizon of universalism but remains European. The good European seeks to reactivate his own identity in a contrasting way, while also refusing the idea that Europe's unity should become cosmopolitan.[31] In the same work, Nietzsche writes: "the cultural concept of 'Europe' does not include all of geographical Europe; it includes only those nations and ethnic minorities who possess a common past in Greece, Rome, Judaism, and Christianity."[32] With the highly notable exception of Judaism, the Romanticism of the German Historical School is reflected in this definition. Jacob Burckhardt, with his roots in the Hegelian tradition of history, would agree with Nietzsche's method of selection here, although the art historian of Basel would not have included Judaism as a component of cultural tension any more than he would have been capable of shedding his nostalgic view of antiquity.

It is therefore not by chance but rather by logical compositional choice that Nietzsche opens this same part 8 of *Beyond Good and Evil* with a kind of biographical confession written in the first person. The previous two parts of the book play consistently with the personal pronouns "us," the plural "you," and "I." It also comes as no surprise that the reflections on Europe in "People and Fatherlands" are bracketed by aphorisms on music, since Nietzsche himself says that music is the *Spätling* (latecomer) of a culture, and that it appears "in the autumn and deliquescence of the culture to which it belongs: at a time when the first signs and harbingers of a new spring are as a rule already perceptible."[33] This is further explained by the fact that Nietzsche considers German music "the music of Europe,"[34] as it expresses the havoc wreaked on Europe by classicism, the Enlightenment, the Revolution, the wars of liberation, and the collapse of the Holy Roman Empire. Moreover, the ground on which Wagner's music was born is the very same on which "a certain *catholicity of feeling* together with a joy in everything *primevally national* came into flower and exuded a mingled odor over Europe: both of which directions of sensibility, comprehended in their greatest intensity and pursued to their farthest limits, finally became audible in the art of Wagner"[35]—particularly *Parsifal* and *Siegfried* . . .

Gut deutsch sein, heißt sich entdeutschen,[36] written by a German, might be seen as resembling the Epimenides paradox. Yet such a position quickly forgets that Nietzsche does not exclude the possibility of being a proper German in this phrase—indeed, for him, this is exactly what one must seek to be: "one should not be afraid to proclaim oneself simply a *good European* and actively to work for the amalgamation of nations: wherein the Germans are, through their ancient and tested quality of being the *interpreter and mediator between peoples*, able to be of assistance."[37] This final turn of phrase is an ironic accusation directed at anti-Semites, who often used such classifications to define the role that they wanted to assign to Jews.

From aphorism 240 to aphorism 247, Nietzsche pursues multiple sonic registers of reflection:

a) The baseline is devoted to German music. In aphorisms 246 and 247, he changes tones to move toward an aesthetics in the etymological sense of the word, meaning the perception of sentient affects, the tendency to listen closely, and therefore, to read and write well: "everyone who is a good European now has to learn *to write well and even better*: this is still so even if he happens to have been born in Germany." Writing better contributes to the accomplishment of what the good Europeans consider "their great task: the direction and supervision of the total culture of the earth.— Whoever preaches the opposite and sets no store by writing well and reading well [. . .] is in fact showing the peoples a way of becoming more and more *national*: he is augmenting the sickness of this century and is an enemy of all good Europeans, an enemy of all free spirits."[38]

b) The melodic theme is clearly a critique of patriotism and the tendency to regress toward atavistic regionalism. Behind civilization and democratization lies a uniformization that ceaselessly triggers fierce reactions, such that this movement of civilization (and not culture) results in the "cultivation of tyrants."[39]

c) The dominant tone thus enables us to become aware of the deep antagonism between culture and civilization, an omnipresent theme in the unpublished fragments starting in 1887.[40] This is no surprise, as Nietzsche makes of this the ambiguity of the moderns. Aphorism 22 of *The Antichrist* sums up this antagonism: civilization, which entails uniformization and domestication, is opposed to culture, which is full of growth as well as degeneracy and thus reflects a true dynamic of values, while civilization feebly attempts to solidify values by hypostasizing them and pronouncing their content unchangeable. It is also for this reason that if America is considered Europe's child, it is seen to be lacking a sense of studious ease[41]—to such a degree that it develops a form of barbarism that poses a threat to Europe as well:[42] "Looking for work in order to be paid: in civilized countries today almost all men are equal in doing that. For all of them work is a means and not an end in itself."[43]

Yet the antagonism between culture and civilization is necessary in order to highlight the limits of the conflicts proper to each culture, to reactivate them and overcome national singularities and cultural identities. This reactivation is possible only if we position ourselves at the very heart of a national culture and its identity—that is, within its language. This overcoming of the decline of nations cannot have an abstract universalism as its goal. Any horizon of this kind, for the Germans, takes the form first and foremost of the Napoleonic victories, imposing the universal power of France and the Revolution. Instead, its goal must be Europe as a battlefield on which the great enemies confront one another, Plato against Homer, and all the modern versions of what Nietzsche calls this "true" antagonism.[44] Europe is not a political horizon authorizing a confederation of states; it is, rather, what allows every good German—and the same goes for all other cultural identities—to degermanize themselves without leaving the battlefield, without leaping to the irenic plane of universal and fraternal harmony. It is also the horizon that is defined by rising values. Nietzsche's viewpoint, beyond the disagreements between "nationalists," is that "for the spiritual flattening of a people there is a compensation, namely the deepening of another people."[45] Of course, there is a great risk here that Europe might be considered an "organism" in the way that the Historical School and the Romantics saw it. However, Nietzsche attaches it more concretely to the idea of the conservation of energy, which can be found in the background of his justifications of the "will to power" on the basis of physics. This idea is perfectly compatible with the idea of the eternal return, although it is less so with the notion of prodigious virtue as well as that of the tragic, which presupposes a real expenditure and loss of energy without any compensation. The general economy of values depends upon the fluctuations of the "will to power," which seem to follow the rules of a zero-sum game.

Aphorisms 248 and 249 compose a crescendo, a double pause before a crash of cymbals. The first of these two aphorisms presents, in the form of a specific duality, an internal tension within what appear to be the temperaments of peoples—at least those endowed with genius . . . Accordingly, there are feminine temperaments and masculine temperaments: the Greeks and the French are feminine, while the Jews, the Romans, and of course the Germans are masculine. These two poles, which take part in life and culture, attract one another and in so doing make mistakes about one another:

a) misunderstandings, like understandings, and in the same way as them, are actors in the dynamic of cultures;
b) these tensions are, of course, deeper—that is, more active than the contingent national distinctions of the political order. The precise delimitation of nations is blurred, yet they tend to petrify and solidify the dynamic between pairs or trios of peoples.

Aphorism 249 grants to the "people with the best Tartuffes" that it does not possess a monopoly on hypocrisy—rather, this is equally shared among all of them. Our virtues are our tartufferies, which we can denounce without knowing, nonetheless, what is best within ourselves, our true virtues—our true "excellences" (ἀρεταὶ) for we cannot be our best selves alone, but only in relation, in interactions that are already caught up in a dynamic. Nietzsche stages an opposition between *having*—the virtues we ascribe to ourselves and claim as our heritage—and *being*—the best that we do not know but embody. Having is located on the side of the "bourgeoisie," of capitalism, assets, nation, and Goethean *Bildung*. Being is, of course, on the side of the "aristocracy," nobility, and action.

The viewpoint of the critique of nations is presented in the following way: the vision of Europe as composed of dynamic relations characterizes Europe as what it is—i.e., what it will be or may become. But this critique does not come from the standpoint of *having*, of a form of possession considered superior, which would amount to a lapse into tartuffery. Rather, it emerges from the nobility that means being what one is without being that alone, entailing the existence of becoming. What is *vornehm* (noble) is self-respect in all ignorance of one's best qualities, which Nietzsche calls, in an ironically secularized sense—faith.[46]

The crash of cymbals in aphorism 250 and particularly aphorism 251 (one of the longest in part 8) consists in positioning Jews—that is, mainly, German Jews—as a determining component of the group destined to take charge of Europe. In other words, the group of free spirits responsible for the cultural dynamic that will overcome the rigid traditions of given national identities and heritages. The fact that Jews are present in the context of this reflection on Europe in a contrasting way should come as no surprise after reading aphorism 249. At the same time, Nietzsche does not position himself as an extremely pro-Semitic figure; he watches the spectacle as a philosopher and an artist. Being both a philosopher and an artist—without being taken over by one aspect or the other or having them fuse completely as in the Romantic and Schopenhauerian tradition—means holding the deepest antagonism within oneself, the one that divides Plato from Homer. And we must remember that "If Christianity has done everything to orientalize the occident, Judaism has always played an essential part in occidentalizing it again: which in a certain sense means making of Europe's mission and history a *continuation of the Greek*."[47] The Jews thus reserve the right to a special recognition—even if it is not entirely equitable toward medieval Islam (but is Nietzsche's really a historians' history?), especially since "As soon as it is no longer a question of the conserving of nations but of the production of the strongest possible European mixed race, the Jew will be just as usable and desirable as an ingredient of it as any other national residue."[48]

When Nietzsche published *Beyond Good and Evil* in 1886, he was fully aware that his attack on Heinrich von Treitschke came in the aftermath of a controversy begun in 1880 by the latter's 1879 article in *Preußischen Jahrbüchern*, "Unsere Ansichten," which had provoked an official response of outrage from seventy-five professors at the University of Berlin spearheaded by . . . Theodor Mommsen. Von Treitschke's anti-Semitism was racialized; it was as a result of physical characteristics he attributed to Jews that he considered it unlikely if not impossible for them to be integrated into Germany: "they [Jews] should become Germans. They should feel themselves, modestly and properly, Germans—and this without prejudicing their faith and their ancient, holy memories, which we all hold in reverence. For we do not want to see millennia of Germanic morality followed by an era of German-Jewish hybrid culture."[49] This line of questioning, which might seem to be aimed at the capacity for assimilation, is indeed informed by a true anti-Semitism: "It would be sinful to forget that a great many Jews, baptized and unbaptized, were German men in the best sense. Felix Mendelssohn, Veit, Riesser, etc.—to say nothing of the living—were men in whom we honor the noble and good traits of the German spirit."[50] Of course, Treitschke does not remain at the level of intellectual characteristics or cultural specificities and reveals the depth of his racism, at least in private, in a letter to his wife dating from the autumn of 1879: "The main difference is in the eyes [. . .] and in the hips, which are the pride of the German peoples."[51] His brutality did not lead him to denounce emancipation or prevent it in the future, but rather, for him, it was a question of a kind of grace that the Germans were to grant the Jews "in the hope that the Jews will strive to be like their fellow citizens." The Jews should feel indebted to the young German nation, "for participation in the State is by no means a natural right of all residents since each State decides on this according to its free judgment." We must remember that the Jews, however, had no access to public employment or to the higher levels of the state, and even less to those of the army. Emancipation in Germany did not make Jews full citizens as it did in France. When Nietzsche writes that he has "not met a German yet who was well disposed toward the Jews,"[52] he is not simply reflecting a certain anti-Semitic reaction proper to the Bismarck-era *Kulturkampf*, but rather posing the specifically German problem of Jewish integration in all its seriousness. Wilhelm Marr founded the League of Anti-Semites in 1879; Ernst Henrici organized the anticonservative and anti-Semitic Soziale Reichspartei; Max Liebermann and Bernhard Förster created the Deutscher Volksverein in 1881, the same year that the Szczecinek Neustettin synagogue in Pomerania was burned down during a violent protest. The German Anti-Semitic Union (which claimed to be socialist, democratic, and liberal) was founded in 1884; the first deputy with an explicitly anti-Semitic agenda, Otto Böckel, was elected to the Reichstag in 1891. In the town of Xanten in the Rhineland, accusations of ritual murder emerged, and the following year, the same thing happened in Konitz in Prussia.

In this context, to assert in 1885 that "The Jews [. . .] are beyond any doubt the strongest, toughest, and purest race now living in Europe"[53] is more than a mere reactive provocation. Likewise, to claim that Jews and Russians are the "surest and most probable factors in the great play and fight of forces"[54] does not demonstrate a predictive clarity. Rather, Nietzsche chooses the two peoples that the Germany of his time systematically excluded from the geopolitical arena to better illustrate the idea that the "'nation' [. . .] is really rather a *res facta* than a *res nata* (and occasionally can hardly be told from a *res ficta et picta*)."[55] In any case, Europe's program to integrate the Jews (which, as Nietzsche understands well, implies an "attenuation of the Jewish instincts") goes hand in hand with the proposal to "expel the anti-Semitic screamers from the country."[56]

The end of aphorism 251 should be emphasized, as Nietzsche "break[s] off"[57] here, asserting while doing so that if he were to continue, he would say what he truly believes: "let silence be the general rule, or let only what is necessary be said, and in few words."[58] It falls to the reader to reflect—to suspend the *staccato* of the text in favor of the *lento* of the spirit.

In aphorism 252, Nietzsche is so critical of the English that it is almost impossible not to detect, in the negative, a profound attachment to German philosophy (which resonates quite naturally with the idea elaborated in aphorism 87 of "The Wanderer and His Shadow"). Nietzsche mobilizes Kant against Hume, Schelling against Locke, and reunites Hegel and Schopenhauer, "these two hostile brother geniuses" against empiricist pragmatism and utilitarianism.[59] Seeing so many of Nietzsche's usual targets enlisted against Albion can only elicit a smile. The new group that Nietzsche calls upon to govern Europe will not be driven by English philosophy, for, in Europe, "the farther west we go [. . .] higher culture can no longer allow its fruits to mature. From lack of repose our civilization is turning into a new barbarism."[60]

This is a *pro domo* appeal, which is extended, in aphorism 253, to a conflict between the Germanic male temperament and its feminine counterpart, France, seduced by "modern ideas" and starstruck by "Anglomania."[61] The result is a bitter scene within the strong European couple. The same France that invented "*noblesse* [. . .] in every higher sense" (that is, not in the trivial sense of Gotha) was led astray by a British Léon Dupuis.[62]

The music of the future, too, must be more than European—that is, more than Franco-German, even including parts of North Africa.[63] We can think of Debussy and Ravel, but also Schönberg, if we consider that the composition of *Beyond Good and Evil* signified the establishment of unresolved dissonances. Europe, in short, is a horizon of overcoming and the symbol of a dynamic of the reactivation of tensions, as well as a springboard toward the South—not toward Nordic values. Music as well, in this context, is a metaphor for the general tonality of a way of living: the symbolic language of a certain style of "will to power."

The conclusion of the chapter gathers all the momentum developed in it, underlining certain aspects in a more pointed way before closing with a poem—a true sonorous caricature of the music of the master of Bayreuth. This poem turns Wagner against himself, trapping him with his own projected image of legitimacy: *Parsifal* is no longer Germany, it is already Rome, the reanimated nostalgia for the Holy Roman Empire so dear to Novalis and the Romantics. Meanwhile the real Germany, which Wagner betrays, is embodied by Siegfried, a more rough and barbarous figure than the French could ever embody. Siegfried is directly associated with freedom and severity—qualities that drive Nietzsche to call himself the philosopher of the Antichrist; in other words, he who does not rush to prostrate himself at the foot of the cross like Delacroix or Wagner. And it is through the composition of *Siegfried* that Wagner exercised "*supra-German* sources and impulses."[64]

Once again, Nietzsche's seemingly excessive praise of Siegfried is evidence not of any regret or nostalgia but rather of the will to heighten the tension within the couple composed of Germany and France, making of Siegfried's anti-Latin temperament the very cause of a crescendo in the antagonism with the Mediterranean world so lauded in the previous aphorism. Just as the strongest critique is the one that adopts not an external viewpoint but an immanent one, a cultural temperament is all the weaker if it is subsumed under an exterior influence (like the seduction of France by the English or by Schopenhauer). We must understand Nietzsche's thinking against Wagner through Wagner's own work as a methodological lesson.

Aiming for European unity means opposing "nationalist madness." Yet succumbing to the mirage of unity means falling back into nostalgia in the manner of a Novalis figure. Nietzsche's Europe moves not in the direction of cosmopolitanism but rather toward the heightened confrontation of free spirits from within each of its cultural components.

"The Purest Race
in Europe . . ."

Among the German philosophers of the nineteenth century, Nietzsche, along with Schelling, was one of the rare thinkers to express such an unaggressive and indeed benevolent attitude toward Jews. His vicious attacks on Christianity and the hunger for power on the part of priests of all creeds cast an ambiguous light on this goodwill. We know what a cutting critique Nietzsche directed at the figure of Paul,[1] who "remained Saul,"[2] just as Christianity is a product of Judaism.[3] Between ambivalence and ambiguity, the reception of Nietzsche has often opted to claim his complicity by linking the man and his thought to anti-Semitism, especially as the Nazis, at least for a time, seem to have held him in high esteem, thus affirming such a thesis, albeit debatably. The vagueness around Nietzsche's reception has indeed taken advantage of the thinker's ambiguity, which has proven compromising on multiple levels, as his declarations of war against all democratic, socialist, and anarchist movements resonate with the characteristics traditionally attributed to the far right. This charge upholds, moreover, the accusation of Nietzsche's "racialization"[4] of the entirety of political, social, and cultural dynamics to the extent that he considers them as "using the body as a guide."[5]

It is true, in any case, that in his youth, between the

ages of twenty-five and thirty, Nietzsche was under the influence of his worship of Schopenhauer, who cannot be considered a supporter of Jews,[6] as well as of his fascination with Wagner, born of a true admiration for the incontestably innovative and socially recognized composer. Wagner opened a much more prominent social world to Nietzsche, the young professor at Basel who had known only the very rural towns of Röcken and Naumburg, despite the prestigious position his father briefly held. It seems that at that time Nietzsche adopted Wagner and his wife's anti-Semitic opinions, perhaps less out of conviction than social cowardice. It is clear that the opposition he stages at the end of chapter 9 of *The Birth of Tragedy* between Aryans and Semites relates to the way in which each "people" represents sacrilege and sin in personified form, and he does not bring any derogatory judgment to bear on the position of "Semites." When he writes to Wagner in May 1869 to express his "gratitude" and "reverence," he praises the Wagnerian "worldview" for resisting "all sorts of political calamities, philosophical mischief and obtrusive Jewry"[7]— this last is thus not the only factor in the attenuation of the "German soul." A letter to his friend Gersdorff of the following March clearly demonstrates that "Judaism" is a generic term that has no direct relation to the historical and phenomenal reality of reformed Judaism: "Our 'Jews'—and you know how embracing that concept is—particularly hate Wagner's idealistic cast of mind, which is what relates him most closely to Schiller: this glowing highhearted struggle for the dawning of the 'day when men shall be noble.'"[8] There is quite a striking contrast when we consider, on the one hand, the letter to his mother of October 1, 1872, where, in describing a journey in Switzerland, Nietzsche complains about the presence of a Jew in his hotel, and, on the other, his letter to Shlomo Lipiner of August 1877, where the reversal of his position is evident: "I have recently had *quite* a few experiences that aroused a *great deal of* expectation, especially from youngsters of this origin."[9]

Between these letters, Nietzsche's friendship with Wagner had ended. Yet Nietzsche's position was not simply reactive. His interest in Paul Rée's "psychological" work deepened, despite Cosima Wagner's violent objections. In the April issue of *Bayreuther Blätter*, Wagner had indirectly referred to *Human, All Too Human*, using his article "Public and Popularity" to attack German authors who tried to imitate the French and treat "the German language as an instrument of virtuosity."[10] In a letter to Marie von Schleinitz, Cosima Wagner proves herself to be more brutal: "Last of all Jewry, in the person of one Dr. Rée [. . .] to all appearance entirely influenced and dominated by Nietzsche, but in reality making a dupe of him, an illustration on a small scale of the relation between Judea and Germania."[11] Following this, Nietzsche is unequivocal in his opposition to anti-Semitism, as multiple letters attest, including his letter of March 29, 1887, to the editor Theodor Fritsch[12] as well as that of February 3, 1888, to Franz Overbeck. Moreover, Nietzsche was personally confronted by an avowed anti-Semite, namely, his own brother-in-law.[13] Nietzsche's attitude could not have been clearer: he refused not only to attend his sister's wedding, but also to respond to her repeated requests for money to compensate for her husband's bankruptcy after his failed attempt to found a colony in Paraguay based on the principle of Aryan purity ("Nueva Germania"). While Elisabeth was christened "queen of New Germany," her husband gave in to the pressure of the difficulties he encountered and committed suicide in June of 1889.

It is thus clear that over the course of the second half of the 1870s, Nietzsche broke with the ordinary German atmosphere in general, but most prominently with the two masters of his youth, Schopenhauer and Wagner,[14] to follow a personal path in which his stances would no longer be determined by motivations at the biographical level. When it comes down to it, had Nietzsche been an anti-Semite, he would not have been prevented from expressing this in one way or another, given that the general environment was so conducive to such heinous declarations.[15] Nietzsche's first important declaration on this matter after his independence from Wagner's circle is found in aphorism 475 of *Human, All Too Human*. While we do see a stereotype of the time here—the figure of the "stock-exchange Jew"—this reference to a socioprofessional reality is taken up in the context of a more general reflection: "Every nation [. . .] possesses unpleasant, indeed dangerous qualities: it is cruel to demand that the Jew should constitute an exception."[16] This praise paean is particularly striking as, for Nietzsche, Jews are those who gave Europe "the noblest human being (Christ), the purest sage (Spinoza), the mightiest book and the most efficacious moral code in the world."[17] What is more, the Jews are those who have essentially achieved "unmythical elucidation" and maintain an aspiration to the Enlightenment and spiritual independence—"If Christianity has done everything to orientalize the occident, Judaism has always played an essential part in occidentalizing it again." Nietzsche relates the "Jewish question" to the intensified nationalisms that resist the formation of "the strongest possible European mixed race" and spread "the literary indecency of leading the Jews to the sacrificial slaughter as scapegoats for every possible public or private misfortune."[18] Here we can almost hear the echo of the famous passage of Rousseau's *Profession of Faith of a Savoyard Vicar*, with the difference that Rousseau insisted that public discussion of the "Jewish question" should not cease until the Jews had their own state. This position would be untenable for Nietzsche in general, and here in particular, as he closes aphorism 473 with an injunction that he will never retract, although he never subscribed to an anarchist doctrine: "*as little state as possible*."[19] Furthermore, it is quite clear that despite his benevolence, which was rare and even exceptional in Germany at a time when the Prussian Reich was so unified and triumphant, Nietzsche speaks *of* Judaism and *of* the Jew as "just as usable and desirable as an ingredient [. . .] as any other national residue."[20] In other words, "Judaism" and "Jews" are less *realia* than notions called to participate in a battle between giants of cultural forces mobilized by a history that, in becoming predictive, ceases to be historical. Nietzsche's statements that are formulaic and accordingly effective—such as "orientaliz[ing] the occident"—can only be called probable opinions. We know very well that for Nietzsche, Christ does not remain a noble figure for long, and that Spinoza will soon no longer represent wisdom. Indeed, at the time, Nietzsche had hardly read Spinoza, and the biblical moral code would be presented as the paradigm of a *pia fraus* and a deceptive inversion of values. It is worth noting that when Nietzsche invokes Jerusalem (about four times in his body of work), he praises strictly nonspecific virtues: "Paris, Provence, Florence, Jerusalem, Athens—these names prove something: genius *depends* on dry air, on clear skies."[21] Yet Nietzsche never set foot in Jerusalem or Paris, let alone Athens: geography here becomes metaphorical, and climate becomes allegorical. This is the same way he seems to treat the terms "Judaism" and "Jewish." In short, his avowed pro-Semitism rests essentially on . . . ignorance of what he praises.

Nietzsche's other significant text specifically devoted to the Jewish people, titled "On the People of Israel," is aphorism 205 of *Dawn*. Here again, we see his emphatic rejection of the small Wagnerian world, if this emphasis was needed. But the opening of the text, despite its initial irony, locates Nietzsche's thought on a level where it will remain for the rest of his life on the question of Jews. This is the level of the "philosophy of history." Speaking about the "coming century," Nietzsche positions himself as a prophet, observing a current reality so as to predict certain developments already in progress. He expresses his prediction in terms of an alternative: "either to become Europe's masters or to lose Europe."[22] This alternative is expressly framed as the same one that faced the Jews in ancient Egypt. The question is reformulated in terms of a history and sociology of culture. Losing Europe does not mean leading Europe to its end, but being banished as the Jews were when they left Egypt—our retrospective viewpoint should not mislead us to confirm the statement of the self-proclaimed "poet-prophet," but should encourage us to observe how Nietzsche, without hesitation, decides the fate of a people to which he does not attribute their own dynamic. The praise for Jewish values that he expresses, once again, exceptional for the time, should not obscure the deeper motives of such a homage: the Jews have "managed to create for themselves a feeling of power and of eternal vengeance out of the very businesses that had been handed over to them (or to which one had handed them over)."[23] The fact that the Jews are destined to produce "great people and great works"[24] can already be observed in nineteenth-century Germany, as well as their search for an "[alliance with] Europe's best nobility"[25]—a theme Nietzsche takes up again several years later in *Beyond Good and Evil*. Yet above all, Nietzsche is fighting exclusively for a specific development of the Jewish condition: assimilation.[26]

This aphorism of *Dawn* (aphorism 205) is contemporaneous with the pogroms in Odessa. Three years later, in 1884, Leon Pinsker published *Auto-Emancipation* in Berlin. Nietzsche was unaware of this, just as he knew nothing of the First Aliyah, or Eliezer Ben-Yehuda's effort to establish "modern" Hebrew—both these events were simultaneous with the publication of *Dawn*. For Nietzsche, the assimilation of the Jews was a self-evident process, which, at the same time, diminished the significance of this phenomenon's historical reality in his view. This explains the coexistence, within these texts, of praiseful goodwill and of certain stereotypes, which indeed appear contradictory. Nietzsche references "crooked [. . .] noses"[27] and "obsequiousness" as well as "[importunity]" in the same breath as he speaks of "mental suppleness," "shrewdness,"[28] domestic virtues, and the tradition of knowledge of which Jews must constantly remind their fellow Europeans.[29] Such a double perspective evinces an attitude that grounds its benevolence in an ignorance of the history of the people in question. Nietzsche knew nothing of Kabbalah, of the mysticism of Isaac Luria, of Sabbatean convulsions, of the conflict between the Hasidim and the Misnagdim—in brief, of all that could have qualified his proclaimed appreciation for Jewish "rationalism."[30] Nor did he know anything about the socioprofessional consequences for Jews of the restrictions imposed on them from access to public works, higher education, and military status. As he mentions, he was aware that Treitschke had demanded the Jews' radical abandonment of any links to their tradition and heritage, all while casting doubt on their capacity to assimilate, even physically. These declarations caused a scandal at the University of Berlin where, under the auspices of Mommsen (the only one who was not Jewish . . .), fifty professors signed a petition in January 1880 opposing Treitschke's remarks. This, however, did nothing to overturn the obligation to convert to Christianity in order obtain a professorship or, in the exceptional cases where this status was attained, as in the cases of Georg Simmel and Hermann Cohen, in order to be invited to other universities, the normalized development of a professorial career. The persistence of these stereotypes in Nietzsche's work, both positive and negative, clearly shows us that "the Jews" were a category more of cultural reflection than of social reality, and that certain characteristics were attributed to this category in accordance with motives that had very little to do with its historical referent. When benevolence is the dominant attitude, pejorative characteristics are presented as at best anomalies in relation to the general type, which is not presented as artificial. This goodwill, with its exceptional status, thinks it is excused from taking a step toward a true knowledge of the people; Nietzsche thus exempts himself from this additional effort. This is not a properly philosophical position; nor is the reluctance to consider the question of assimilation on the level of law.

A "material" civil law is, in fact, an antinomy since there is no criterion in formal law that allows for the measure of a citizen's adherence (demanded by Treitschke) to any confession of faith in a state that does not have such a confession of faith in its constitution. But the question of the relation between formal and "material" law leads Nietzsche into "Socratic" discussions that end with his having to admit to presuppositions he initially denied and of which he contests the very validity.[31] For Nietzsche, "formal validity" is at worst a crude error and at best a *pia fraus*, an "intellectual sublimation." It can even be a ruse intended to achieve personal gain in an economy of power, whether enacted by the "weak" or the "strong." For example, Nietzsche critiques the way in which Christianity, through its interpretation of the Old Testament,[32] deformed the meaning of the text for its own benefit, and he emphatically praises the style of the Old Testament in comparison with the rococo texts of the New Testament.[33] Yet the difficulty and fragility of this position become clear when we consider that Nietzsche also considers the Jews the inventors of Christianity;[34] and if they "brought moral sublimity to its climax,"[35] it is also with this people that "the slave revolt in morals" began—it is they who "brought off that miraculous feat of an inversion of values [. . .] using the word 'poor' as synonymous with 'holy.'"[36] According to Nietzsche, by "[de-deifying]" the word "world," the Jews established anti-nature (a synonym for morality),[37] which spread by way of Christianity. Its central tenet was the negation of the world, the will to change the individual although he is but "a slice of fate [. . .] one more law, one more necessity." To ask him to obey rules decreed by a certain vision of how life should be would mean "insisting that everything should change, even retroactively."[38]

In the twentieth-century reception of Nietzsche, it is common to claim that the philosopher often contradicted himself and that for each assertion he made, there was an opposite assertion.[39] In such a reading of the role of Jews for Nietzsche, aphorism 475 of *Human, All Too Human*, where he credits them with "orientalizing the occident," would be refuted by aphorism 141 of *The Gay Science*, titled "Too Oriental," which excoriates the concept of a god "who casts an evil eye and threats upon anyone who does not believe in [his] love[.] What? A love encapsulated in if-clauses attributed to an almighty god?"[40] On the one hand, Nietzsche's philosophy has its own history and a specific evolution that we must take into account in the process of identifying its essential aspects. On the other hand, the decisive and well-known conception formulated in the phrase "will to power" must be understood in terms of its intrinsic consequences as well as the ways it is applied to what Nietzsche calls "world history," which he opposes to "essential history."[41] The latter precedes and determines the former despite all our illusions—of which the least easy to eradicate would consider the individual precisely *not* to be reducible to a "slice of fate." This clear opposition between two "histories," or rather, two modalities of historicity, is not new in Nietzsche's thought: it goes back, not to the second "Untimely Observation," but to the posthumously published text written in 1873 and never renounced by the author, "On Truth and Lie in an Extramoral Sense," where Nietzsche develops the fable of the invention of knowledge: "That was the highest and most mendacious minute of 'world history'—yet only a minute."[42] Nietzsche takes care, here, to put "world history" in quotation marks. This is thus an indirect "quotation" of a *topos*, and these quotation marks express the ironic distance with which Nietzsche returns to this term, so powerful in nineteenth-century Germany. This "world history" is interpreted as the creation of the "clever animals" who invented knowledge, and thus as one of their illusions. World history, in this early text, is already denounced as a false representation in relation to what is essential: cosmic forces, the unyielding logic of the natural dynamic.

The intuition of the "will to power" arose in the autumn of 1880, followed, in 1881, by the "revelation" of the eternal return, that is, despite numerous signs, *after* the composition of the first works Nietzsche wrote in the aftermath of his freedom from the Wagner circle and his break from the Schopenhauerian conception of the "will." During the turning point of 1880–81, Nietzsche had not yet drawn all the consequences of his new philosophical constellation. A theory of "instincts" and drives is expressed to us as a world regulated exclusively by conflicts between "forces," that is, dynamics of energy in permanent convulsion, which do not give rise to infinite possible configurations, as the overall quantum of energy remains constant.[43] There is thus indeed "eternal return," but not yet in the provocative (and exoteric) form that Nietzsche chose for the last four books of *The Gay Science* in the summer of 1882.[44]

On the Genealogy of Morals undertakes the project of direct explanation with the explicit didactic goal of demonstrating the meaning of essential history by means of examples from world history as Nietzsche chooses to reconstitute it. But the two works of 1888, *Twilight of the Idols* and *The Antichrist*, reveal the true consequences of Nietzsche's earliest articulation of the "will to power." Namely, the eternal return on the plane of history *per se*, at last decipherable after the dissipation of all our illusions that still cling to world history. At the end of European nihilism, marked by a long phase of decadence (Christianity, as the Judaism of the priesthood, accompanied by "Socratism," rejecting its prerequisite Hellenism),[45] we arrive at the *conversion of values*.

Beginning with *Dawn*, we must understand the reasons for Nietzsche's apparent ambivalence in his judgment on the Jews in accordance with this concept of conversion of values: "What Europe owes to the Jews? Many things, good and bad, and above all one thing that is both of the best and of the worst: the grand style in morality, the terribleness and majesty of infinite demands, [. . .] the whole romanticism and sublimity of moral questionabilities."[46] The "recognition" that Nietzsche speaks of with regard to Jews is, however, simply a "spectacle" (an expression of world history) that they offer against the background of an "evening sky" (the end of European decadence) which is "burning now—perhaps burning itself out," a spectacle witnessed by "artists [. . .] and philosophers," those who know of the coming conversion of values.[47] In this context, we can better understand the logic by which Nietzsche calls Jews "the *most disastrous* people in world history."[48] This pronouncement is made, for him, from the viewpoint of the effects on world history of the configuration to which they belong, *like other peoples*, within the order of essential history: "There are two types of genius: one which above all begets and wants to beget, and another which prefers being fertilized and giving birth. Just so, there are among peoples of genius those to whom the woman's problem of pregnancy and the secret task of forming, maturing, and perfecting has been allotted [. . .] and others who must fertilize and become the causes of new orders of life—like the Jews, the Romans, and, asking this in all modesty, the Germans?"[49] Two aphorisms later, Nietzsche attacks German anti-Semitism head-on, railing against "anti-Jewish [. . .] stupidity" while also admitting that he is writing about "matters that are none of my business."[50] His avowed aim here is that of resistance against the vague nationalists and protectionists who opposed the immigration of Jews from Eastern Europe. The slogan of such bigoted people was "Admit no more Jews"—a slogan Nietzsche refutes with the argument that the Germans are "a nation whose type is still weak and indefinite and that fears that a stronger race will come and blur or extinguish it. Now the Jews are beyond any doubt the strongest, toughest, and purest race now living in Europe."[51] The term "nation," here used as a synonym for "race," as was common at the time, is also held under suspicion when it "can hardly be told [apart] from a *res ficta et picta* [a fiction]."[52] The meaning of "nation" in this context is immediately opposed to another sense of the term "race": a less inchoative reality, and indeed, the final stage of sedimentation, which is more resistant from the perspective of world history because it is more grounded in the essential history of configurations of power. The Jews, like the Romans, represent a more ancient form of "genius"—the difference being that the Romans disappeared from the historical stage, while the Jews remained. While it is necessary to "expel the anti-Semitic screamers from the country," Nietzsche says, Jews should be "accommodated with all caution, with selection; approximately as the English nobility does."[53] As he did five years earlier in *Dawn*, Nietzsche extols hybridization with "nobility from the March Brandenburg," where he speculates that the Jews could introduce "a little spirituality, which is utterly lacking among these officers."[54] The irony is evident, but stereotypes are upheld (the text mentions "the genius of patience and money" with respect to

Jews). The end of the aphorism moves the "Jewish question" entirely beyond the terrain of German problems regarding the integration or exclusion of Jews: "But here it is proper to break off my cheerful Germanomania and holiday oratory; for I am beginning to touch on what is *serious* for me, the 'European problem' as I understand it, the cultivation of a new caste that will rule Europe."[55]

Nietzsche attacks and denounces anti-Semitism . . . in favor of a certain kind of anti-Judaism. He thus proves himself to be an exception once again: nearly the only German philosopher to denounce the "anti-Semitic screamers," whom he wishes to banish, he is also the only one to recognize "Jewish genius" as an essential aspect of a conversion of values destined to free us from a historical condition inaugurated by Jews. This condition consists, in Nietzsche's reading, of anti-nature, sin, and moral sublimity—in sum, Christian decadence. The hybridization of Jews and the Prussian military which Nietzsche ironically invokes is only a single example, within the frame of world history, of what Nietzsche hopes to see emerge, for the sake of the conversion of values and in accordance with the new embodiment of force. Anti-Semitism, for him, is an effect of weakness within a general movement of decadence. It does not take aim at what Judaism and, as a result, Christianity, which are both more coherent, are responsible for: the refusal of the play of forces, the refusal to "naturalize" the human,[56] the fear of recovering "the terrible, basic text of *homo natura*."[57] For Nietzsche, the "naturalization" of history leads not to a surreptitious conversion of history into nature, but to a determinism of history by "nature," that is, the historicity of energetic configurations, without any ascribable beginning or foreseeable end.

Fear in the face of the world of forces takes numerous forms throughout the course of world history. Nietzsche emphasizes two in particular: "Socratism" and the "priesthood." The latter is an aspect of asceticism, which philosophers are by no means exempt from.[58] This means that the priesthood also goes hand in hand with a specific exertion of force against itself, or more precisely, a sublimated transfer of energy engendering its own "values," which manifest through particular embodied forms, such as the "saint." Indeed, it is before the saint that, he asserts, "so far the most powerful human beings have still bowed worshipfully," finding within this figure's determination "their own strength" of "will." Yet the saint incited "suspicion" with his "enormity of denial, of anti-nature," making them wary of "some very great danger" and arousing "a new fear."[59] Yet while the "ascetic ideal" is anti-natural, it does not negate existence, but attracts many, including the philosopher. Nietzsche explains this by way of the formula *"preat mundus, fiat philosophia, fiat philosophus, fiam!"*[60] This expression holds the key to the reversal of force against the philosopher's own Dionysiac effusion, capable of annihilating its subject. Self-affirmation here is thus a mode of refusal founded on the fear of a loss of self, and is only one manifestation of the "will to power." The saint, the priest, the philosopher—these are all possible appearances of a desire for power that balks in the face of *amor fati* in favor of an enduring illusion: survival in spite of everything. This is how Nietzsche describes what he calls the "morality of *ressentiment*," the most extreme expression of this being the instrumentalization of decadence. And the latter is an irreducible consequence of the natural rhythm alternating between entropy and negentropy in the flux of energy—the "will to power." The Jews become what Nietzsche calls "that priestly people"[61] precisely *after* the ascendant phase in which they professed their "God" to be "a good soldier and a strict judge."[62] They ultimately consider decadence as a means. Thus, from within Judaism itself, Paul and the complex of Christianity arise, which, like the philosophers inspired by Socratism, have "a life-interest in making humanity *sick* and twisting the concepts 'good' and 'evil,' 'true' and 'false.'"[63] We must take care not to mistake the meaning that Nietzsche attributes to the terms "vital" and "life": they are expressions of the "will to power" and not at all of a vitalism attached to the preservation of life in the ordinary sense.[64] It is because the Jewish people were conquered without accepting their defeat that "in opposing their enemies and conquerors [they] were ultimately satisfied with nothing less than a radical revaluation of their enemies' values, that is to say, an act of the *most spiritual revenge*."[65] This, Nietzsche claims, was the only way out for a priestly people.

The long history of this conversion of values has resulted in "our" becoming "dulled to the demand for justice *in historicis*,"[66] just as the "philosophers supported the church: the *lie* of 'the moral world order' runs through the entire development of philosophy, even modern philosophy."[67] But the historical justice Nietzsche lays claim to is historical only with regard to what he calls "essential history," which is, in fact, no longer history *per se* but a form of *fate*, namely, the convulsions of force determined by a general energetics. We might pose the question of the logical foundation of such assertions. For Nietzsche positions himself as the spokesperson—the "prophet," in the Greek etymological sense—"chosen" by the "will to power," which is, by nature, indifferent to any form of individuality. Yet the main point here is the claim of the progressive dissolution of the reality of Judaism and its history—the erasure of its specific contours in favor of an analogy, if not an identity, with the Christian figure of the priest, with the ascetic in general, and, consequently, with the philosopher. The "Jewish question" fades before the dawn of a new conversion of values, in which the Jews will have—at best—fulfilled a role that, once accomplished, will negate their identity along with that of the Christians, under the aegis of the anonymity and ahistoricism of cosmic energies.

The Concept of "Race"

The attempts of Nazi propagandists to enlist Nietzsche's thought for their own purposes all failed for obvious reasons. Nazi idealogue Alfred Rosenberg, in *Der Mythus des 20. Jahrhunderts* (The Myth of the Twentieth Century), maintains that Nietzsche encouraged "the training of the Germanic race to become the superior race."[1] Yet he was unable to explain the philosopher's anti-German stance, his call for a new Europe without national governments, and his attacks on anti-Semites, except by speculating that he must have "fallen into the hands of ambitious politicians."[2] In his book on Nietzsche, Heinrich Härtle, who was entirely representative of the very core of the Nazi doctrine,[3] draws heavily on a lecture by Arno Schickedanz,[4] his colleague at the Amt Rosenberg, which neatly summarizes Hitler's thought. Härtle reproaches Nietzsche for his belief in the assimilation of Jews in the crucible of European civilization, while, in his view, Jews are neither a distinct people nor a race, but a "counter-race," the "parasites of the human species," that is, pathogenic elements who affect, and even compromise, the "clean" race war. It is clear that the theoretical foundation of the "final solution"—long before the Wannsee Conference—was the justification of a "necessary" war against "parasites" since it was a matter of nothing more or less than clearing away one of the recurrent obstacles in history. It was considered necessary to destroy this anti-race precisely because its function was understood as the destruction of races or, at least, the threat of their degeneration. The Nazis thus clearly distinguished the status of Jews: they said that the parasites could not constitute a race that participated in general history in the same manner as others. Furthermore, Nietzsche, an individualist to the point of aristocratism, could "not be a *völkisch* socialist." In addition, as in the case of all the propagandists charged with enlisting Nietzsche, even if only as a precursor to Nazi ideology, Härtle explained that the philosopher "opposes to the Jews the Nordic values of the Greeks, the Romans, and the Germans."[5] To refute this entirely false claim, we need only look to aphorism 248 of *Beyond Good and Evil*:

> There are two types of genius: one which above all begets and wants to beget, and another which prefers being fertilized and giving birth. Just so, there are among peoples of genius those to whom the woman's problem of pregnancy and the secret task of forming, maturing, and perfecting has been allotted—the Greeks, for example, were a people of this type; also the French—and others who must fertilize and become the causes of new orders of life—like the Jews, the Romans, and, asking this in all modesty, the Germans?[6] Peoples, tormented and enchanted by unknown fevers and irresistibly pressed beyond themselves, in love and lusting after foreign races (after those who like "being fertilized"), and at the same time domineering like all that knows itself to be full of creative powers and hence "by the grace of God." These two types of genius seek each other, like man and woman; but they also misunderstand each other—like man and woman.[7]

Here we can observe, on the one hand, that Nietzsche uses the terms "people" and "race" interchangeably; and on the other hand, that the racist Nazi nomenclature does not correspond in any way to the Nietzschean distribution of cultural configurations across these two different paths of genius. And, *last but not least*, it is clear that Nietzsche locates the Jews on the same plane as the Germans in terms of the capacity for genius.

What remains debatable, of course, is Nietzsche's choice of criterion for differentiation. In keeping with his conception of language, it would seem that he is here being at once metaphorical and anthropological, and yet using conceptions that escape historicity, apparently rendered irrelevant by physiological functions.

The discrete substantialization of the "feminine" and the "masculine" displaces the horizon of the "racist" problematic entirely, reinstating cultural history differently, from the viewpoint of the "body" and, thus, of different modes of "sublimation."[8] This indicates that the relation of causality between "races" and "characteristics" of peoples is not at all the terrain on which Nietzsche would develop an anthropology of the evolution of cultures. Therefore, there is no "archi-people" (*Urvolk*) for Nietzsche, as there is for Fichte. No matter what lineage would seem to bind the two, the idea of a "destination," so central for Fichte, is constantly rejected by Nietzsche. In 1811, Fichte writes:

> There are isolated men in world history whose value prevails over millions of others. Divinity is expressed in an unmediated way through a select few among them; for these men alone, the world truly exists. The great majority exist only to serve as instruments, and even this contingent represents a limited number of individuals. The vast majority of this great number only lives to test the others, to unsettle them, to impede them in all possible ways so that they may develop their own power. In the grand order of things, they represent the antithesis and the negative forces which detract so that the affirmative forces, in fighting them, may come to the fore and appear in full daylight.[9]

This passage from Fichte's course in Berlin seems to clearly prefigure the intuition of the "will to power" presiding over human history. Yet, despite this resemblance, Nietzsche would never claim the "minority" of geniuses to be a manifestation of "divinity," nor would he consider that ascendant forces move constantly in the direction of the "daylight" without being condemned to their own inevitable path of decadence. Nor is it a matter, for him, of a secret theodicy, with redemption as the endpoint of this "destination" of geniuses or exceptional beings.[10] Although Nietzsche himself has certain Gnostic aspects, including the idea of ingenious individuals, *beati pauci*, and indeed the "overman," he would never consider the Germans to be the only people moved forward by a special history of which the apocalypse would be the issue. He writes: "Where [. . .] must *we* reach with our hopes? Toward *new philosophers*; there is no choice; toward spirits strong and original enough to provide the stimuli for opposite valuations [. . .]. To teach man the future of man as his *will*, as dependent on a human will, and to prepare great ventures and over-all attempts of discipline and cultivation by way of putting an end to that gruesome dominion of nonsense and accident that has so far been called 'history.'" But this future is by no means guaranteed, for the "frightening danger" remains that these philosopher-kings might "fail to appear or that they might turn out badly or degenerate," while the "monstrous fortuity that has so far had its way and play regarding the future of man—a game in which no hand, and not even a finger, of God took part as a player"— persists, although these exceptional beings "[know] how man is still unexhausted for the greatest possibilities." And "the *over-all degeneration of man* [. . .] this animalization of man into the dwarf animal of equal rights and claims, is *possible*, there is no doubt of it."[11]

A fragment from the summer of 1876 (fragment 17 [55]) provides a kind of prelude to this question of "race." Here, we find the first appearance of the phrase "prejudices about races" (*Rassenvorurteile*): "I imagine future thinkers in whom the European-American restlessness is united with the hundred-times inherited Asiatic contemplativeness: such a combination brings a solution to the world riddle. Meanwhile the observant free spirits have their mission: they remove all the barriers that stand in the way of a blending of human beings: religions states monarchical instincts, illusions of wealth and poverty, prejudices about health and races—etc."[12]

This note, of course, has a biographical context: Nietzsche had recently broken with Wagner and his circle and was becoming close with Paul Rée, who would be his friend until at least 1882. Rée's *Psychological Observations* is cited in *Human, All Too Human*, where Nietzsche says that the author "again and again hit[s] the bullseye."[13] Cosima Wagner's attacks on Rée on the basis of his Judaism played no small role in Nietzsche's break with Wagner, as we have seen. In 1876, Nietzsche asserts, in direct opposition to the anti-Semitic circle of Wagnerians, that he is now in the faction of the "free spirits," committed to combating racial prejudices. Moreover, his refusal to privilege either the *vita activa* or the *vita contemplativa* bears witness to a project that animates Nietzsche's work from this point on: placing himself beyond the choice between modernity (compulsive industriousness) and Christianity (prayerful contemplation), which he suspects of being insidiously at work within what is called modernity, and only a variant of Puritanism. Churches, states, and prejudices about races are thus obstacles to blending and hybridity—that is, to what Nietzsche seeks to establish: a "historical philosophy" that rejects this false opposition between *vita activa* and *vita contemplativa*, for "a mistake in reasoning lies at the bottom of this antithesis [. . .] there exists, strictly speaking, neither an unegoistic action nor completely disinterested contemplation; both are only sublimations [*Sublimierungen*]."[14] This new method of perspectivist historicism, which Nietzsche calls "historical philosophy" or "historical critique," takes on the name "psychological analysis" in the second chapter of *Human, All Too Human* (I, 35), which will soon become "physiology" (I, 10),[15] and Nietzsche speculates that physiology will replace metaphysics.[16] From this viewpoint, all "prejudices about races" are merely temporary and fallacious typologies. However, this strong historical and psychological critique of attitudes regarding "races" does not provide sufficient information on what "race" itself is for Nietzsche, or what constitutes a "race." Nor does it help us to truly understand what lies beyond the opposition between *vita activa* and *vita contemplativa*. At least at that time, Nietzsche considered the "enigma of the world" to exist there—that is, the cultural figure of world history. Consequently, whatever the meaning of the notion of "race" may be, it is situated on the level of a new conception of history that the free spirits must clear the way for. This process begins with the destruction of the illusions of great notions to which nonhistoricist philosophy attributes an undying essence. Yet the enigma of the world cannot be resolved simply through historical or psychological critique as Nietzsche envisions it in the period 1880–81. The elaboration of the "will to power," however, will allow him to go a step further.

We can therefore conclude that what Nietzsche understands as "race" does not coincide with a more contemporary understanding arising from the public sphere. In aphorism 45 of *Human, All Too Human*, I, Nietzsche connects the origin of modern morality and our concepts of "good" and "evil" to the shared values of the "ruling races and castes." But these "ruling races and castes," such as the Greeks and the Trojans (whom he cites as examples), are confronted by oppressed, powerless, and dominated peoples who are also at the origin of values, on the negative side. From the perspective of the powerful, Nietzsche denounces the prevailing notions of "good" and "evil": "Our present morality has grown up on the soil of the *ruling* races and castes."[17] We can thus understand the ironic turn of Nietzsche's presentation. He has no intention of opposing the values of ruling races to those of the oppressed; rather, he is demonstrating the relative nature of inherited values, which are "good" only because they have obliterated all forms of negativity. They can thus be seen as illusions, if we believe that they rely on an effective substratum: "A class, a rank, a race of people, an environment, a contingency— all this is expressed more in a work or act than in a person. [. . .] Conclusion: we should *not* estimate the solitary type in relation to the gregarious type *nor* the gregarious type in relation to the solitary. Seen from above: both are necessary; their antagonism is necessary [. . .] and nothing remains but to dispel this 'desirability,' that is, for some *third* force to develop from the first two ('virtue' as hermaphroditism)."[18]

Although the oppressed are clearly not part of the "ruling races and castes," they belong to what we would call the same "race" as those who oppress them. "Race," then, signifies simply a "social group," or even a part of a "people" or "lineage." Imagining "the coming time of the struggle for world domination," a struggle that will follow "*philosophical doctrines*," Nietzsche specifies that "nations" are "more nuanced concepts than races," even if we "conform to the great principle of kinship based on blood and race."[19] Speaking of a "constitutive element of the German race," Nietzsche points to the "sterility of its aristocracy."[20] In an autobiographical fragment he discusses his Polish heritage and refers to the Germans as having "become one of the most gifted nations only since their blood was strongly mixed with Slavic blood."[21] But his central "political" perspective, in search of "good Europeans," leads him to reject the contemporaneous positions of Bismarck and Wilhelm, that is, the "politics that are desolating the German spirit by making it vain." For, he writes, "[w]e who are homeless are too manifold and mixed racially and in our descent, being 'modern men,' and consequently do not feel tempted to participate in the mendacious racial self-admiration and racial indecency that parades in Germany today as a sign of a German way of thinking and that is doubly false and obscene among people of the 'historical sense.'"[22]

The problem is thus a structural one. There is one "form"—a type of configuration of instincts, drives, and energies—that corresponds to the positioning of the "oppressed" for a certain duration. There is another form that relates to being in the dominant role of a conqueror.[23] In aphorism 13 of the first essay in *On the Genealogy of Morals*, Nietzsche explains this more clearly: "For just as the popular mind separates the lightning from its flash and takes the latter for an *action*, [. . .] so popular morality also separates strength from expressions of strength, as if there were a neutral substratum behind the strong man, which was *free* to express strength or not to do so. But there is no such substratum; there is no 'being' behind doing, effecting, becoming."[24] In other words, the strong man is no more free to become weak someday than the oppressed are to endure their condition.

Nietzsche entirely rejects the idea or hypothesis of "pure races": "There is in all likelihood no such thing as pure races but only races that have become pure and this only with extreme rarity." The Greeks "provide us with the model of a race and a culture that has become pure: and it is to be hoped that one day Europe will also succeed in becoming a pure European race and culture."[25] These "races that have become pure" have triumphed after conflict between discordant qualities. And what within "the mixed races" was "disharmony in physical forms [. . . and] disharmonies in customs and value judgments," generating ill-will, cruelty, and instability, later become strength and beauty. Yet, and this is precisely the point, the Greeks are not a singular "race" but rather a group of populations united around a more or less shared physical condition and common value judgments, irreversibly destined to be dismembered, conquered, and rebuilt in other configurations.

This is the case of all occurrences of the term "race" in Nietzsche's work: the term never denotes the superficial physical qualities attributed to certain populations in the modern sense of genetics.[26] Which is not to say that Nietzsche did not consider the body. On the contrary, the body is highly significant for him, but never in a defined or superficially overdetermined sense aligning in any way with what could be called "ethnic" characteristics. This also does not mean that Nietzsche was unaware of the existence of Black or Asian populations. He mentions "Black" people three times in his work, but always to indicate a capacity to endure suffering greater than that of modern Europeans.[27] In this context, Nietzsche poses the question of the historical and relative nature of what we call "pain" and "suffering."[28] Nietzsche's view of "Asian" people depends on the context in which, in his view, they play a cultural role. This is positive, when, in his estimation, they have a beneficial influence on Europeans.[29] In some cases it is negative, when Nietzsche designates them as those whom the Greeks had to conquer to reach an Apollonian level, while Asia is located at the origin of the Dionysian.[30]

In short, "race" always refers to a cultural configuration (Greek, European), a culture (Romanism), a nation (French, German, English), or a lineage or "caste" that is often transnational or transcultural (leaders, priests, thinkers, artists, warriors, shopkeepers, servers). Moreover, starting in 1881, Nietzsche considers the meaning of "race" to be more subtly expressed through the term "nation."[31] However, without abandoning the period preceding the two years of 1880 and 1881, so decisive for the development of his thought, an aphorism from "Assorted Opinions and Maxims" in *Human, All Too Human* II clearly indicates the path that Nietzsche will never abandon, at least in his published works: he understands "race" as a synonym for "nation."[32]

When, after finishing *Zarathustra*, Nietzsche reconsiders the journey he has just completed during the composition of *Beyond Good and Evil*, his "philosophical genealogy" emerges as constituting at least three stages. These include, first, the "antiteleological" approach and, second, the mechanistic approach—"tracing all

moral and aesthetic questions back to physiological [questions]."
Significantly, however, he doesn't attribute any substantive reality to
matter—and pays homage to Boscovich in this regard. Finally, and
most important, he rejects "the self-mirroring of the mind as a starting point," calling this a "fruitless" path. Rather, he asserts: "I find
no research worth doing unless it uses the body as a guide."[33] From
this viewpoint, what he designates with the term "philosophy" is in
no way a "*dogma*" but "a preliminary guideline for *research*."[34] A body
without matter is interpreted as a kind of force field in which each
force struggles for maximal release. This conflict between energies
results in preliminary configurations that we call bodies:

> Using the body as a guide, we recognize that a human being is a
> multiplicity of animate beings, which sometimes battle one another,
> sometimes are absorbed and subjugated by one another, whenever
> they affirm their individual natures they are also involuntarily af-
> firming the whole.
>
> Among these living beings, there are those who rule to a greater
> degree than they obey, and among these there is again battle and
> victory.
>
> The whole of humankind has all those attributes of that which is
> organic, which we partly remain unconscious of, which we [partly]
> become conscious of in the form of *drives*.[35]

These drives themselves neither remain stable nor occupy a con-
tinuous or selfsame position in the hierarchy to which they are sub-
jected in any given configuration: "Depending on the environment,
and on the conditions under which we live, one drive emerges as the
most highly esteemed and most firmly in command."[36] The "will to
power" manifests as an "expenditure of force"—that is, a conversion
of energy into "life." Up until the last moments of his intellectual
activity, Nietzsche reiterates the necessity of understanding the two
irreversible tendencies constituting the dynamic of what he calls "essential history," linking them together without ever drawing out any
form of "synthesis" between them. On the one hand, there is the
release of forces in the acceptance of the permanent battle between
drives in conflict. On the other, the reaction that this upward motion

elicits manifests in all attempts to contain, delay, and even deny this battle of giants between drives in the service of various forms of stasis, balance, and reconciliation. The idea of "race" in the sense used by anthropologists in the context of any ideology cannot be maintained in the face of what Nietzsche calls "great politics":

> I bring war. *Not* between peoples: I have no words to express my contempt for the European dynasties' abominable politics of interests [. . .]. *Not* between classes [. . .]: those who have the advantage in today's society are physiologically condemned [. . .]. I bring war against all the absurd contingencies of people, class, race, profession, education, culture: a war between rise and fall, between the will to life and *vengefulness* against life.[37]

"Great politics" is founded on physiology in the sense that Nietzsche understands the interpretation of the dynamic of drives. Against all conceptions of finality, this politics seeks to "elevate humanity as a whole," to establish new hierarchies of values on the basis of future capacities offered by "races, peoples, individuals"— with race here signifying "gathering of peoples" (Nietzsche refers to the "European race," for example). The enemy of great politics is "all that is degenerate and parasitic." This clearly does not signify those who are ill or disabled. Rather, the enemy named here consists of all that refuses or depletes the upward movement in which Nietzsche places his hopes, and which he firmly believes will put an end to nihilism. For he diagnoses nihilism as the symptom afflicting his contemporary modernity.

In Fine

After I had sought for a long time to link a certain concept to the word "philosopher," I finally discovered that there are two kinds: (1) those who attempt to *ascertain* an extensive array of facts (2) those who are *lawgivers* of valuations. The former seek to gain control of the world around them, or of a past world, by using signs to summarize what happened: they think it's important to make everything surveyable, categorizable, tangible, accessible—they serve the mission of humans to use all things for their own benefit. But the latter give orders, saying: it shall be so! they are the first to determine the benefits, *what* the benefits are for humanity; they exercise control over the preliminary work of scientific people, but factual knowledge is for them only a means to create.[1]

Acknowledgments

The origin of this book was a conference given at the EHESS (*École des hautes études en sciences sociales*) in Maurice Olender's seminar in 2009. Without his kind and patient support and the inspiration of his work *Race and Erudition*, it would never have been published. For this publication, I have multiple exchanges with my friends Marc Crépon and Pierre Judet de la Combe to thank, as well as the consistent attention of Patricia.

Notes

Introduction

1. Theodor W. Adorno and Thomas Mann, *Correspondence 1943–1955*, ed. Christophe Gödde and Thomas Sprecher, trans. Nicholas Walker (Cambridge, UK: Polity, 2006), 60.

2. Theodor Adorno, "Über Nietzsche und uns" (On Nietzsche and Us), in Max Horkheimer, *Gesammelte Schriften*, vol. 13 (Frankfurt: Fischer, 1989), 111–20. The initial purpose of this interview had been to commemorate the fiftieth anniversary of Nietzsche's death on August 25, 1900.

3. Adorno, "Über Nietzsche und uns," 111–20.

4. Horkheimer displays a certain offhandedness when he identifies Nietzsche's pro-aristocracy stance with a return to feudal values. The only explicit reference to the feudal period in relation to aristocracy in Nietzsche's work is in an aphorism where the "nobility" of free spirits is clearly preferred (*Dawn*, 199); aphorism 201 doesn't leave a trace of doubt, in its conclusion, about the fact that for Nietzsche aristocracy has nothing to do with the register of politics and cannot constitute an object of sociological study (see as well the last chapter of *Beyond Good and Evil*, devoted to "nobility").

5. Adorno, "Über Nietzsche und uns."

6. Adorno, "Über Nietzsche und uns."

7. Alfred Bäumler (1887–1968), *Nietzsche, der Philosoph und Politiker* (Leipzig: Reclam, 1931). On this strange figure, who, prior to Hitler's rise to power, wrote one of the best works on Kant's Third Critique (*Kants Kritik der Urteilskraft*, 2 vols. [Halle: Niemeyer, 1923]), see Max Weinreich's study *Hitler's Professors: The Part of Scholarship in Germany's Crimes against the Jewish People* (New York: YIVO, 1946), as well as Arno Münster's *Nietzsche et le nazisme* (Paris: Kimé, 1998). Cf. as well Rudolf Schottlaender's book *Verfolgte Berliner Wissenschaft*

(Berlin: Hentrich, 1988), analyzed by Maurice Olender in *Race and Erudition*, trans. Marie Jane Todd (Cambridge, MA: Harvard University Press, 2009), 131–33. See also Mazzino Montinari's study, "Nietzsche between Alfred Bäumler and Georg Lukács," in *Reading Nietzsche*, trans. Greg Whitlock (Urbana: University of Illinois Press, 2003 [1982]) as well as Giorgio Colli, *Dopo Nietzsche* (Milan: Adelphi, 1974).

8. Alfred Bäumler also edited a collection of Nietzsche's posthumous works (*Nietzsche. Die Unschuld des Werdens* [Leipzig: Kröner, 1931]). It should be noted that to this day the Kröner edition still includes Alfred Bäumler's presentation of the text, barely amended.

9. This is the phrase (*conversion des valeurs* in French) that we have chosen to render the expression *Umwertung der Werte*, often translated as "transvaluation of values." This concept marks the final stage of Nietzsche's thought, from September 1888 on.

10. This expression appears in Nietzsche's work in 1884. See, for example, fragment 26 [432], summer–autumn 1884, Friedrich Nietzsche, *Unpublished Fragments from the Period of* Thus Spoke Zarathustra *(Spring 1884–Winter 1884/85)*, *The Complete Works of Friedrich Nietzsche*, vol. 15, trans. Paul S. Loeb and David F. Tinsley (Stanford: Stanford University Press, 2022), 246. We will return to this phrase. It is relevant here to bring up the anecdote related by Günther Anders (*Über Heidegger* [Munich: Beck, 2001], 419 ff.) that sets the scene of Hans Jonas and Heidegger walking together after a classical philosophy conference (Bonn, 1969). When Jonas asked him why, in *Being and Time*, he never spoke about the body when discussing the "analytic of *Dasein*," Heidegger's response was: "Indeed, that's what I've always forgotten." Needless to say, this is disarming considering that he devoted the majority of his course to Nietzsche.

11. See, for example, André Comte-Sponville, "The Brute, the Sophist, and the Aesthete: 'Art in the service of an illusion,'" in *Why We Are Not Nietzscheans*, ed. Luc Ferry and Alain Renaut (Chicago: University of Chicago Press, 1997).

12. Nietzsche, *On the Genealogy of Morals*, I, §11; *On the Genealogy of Morals and Ecce Homo*, ed. and trans. Walter Kaufmann (New York: Vintage, 1967), 40–41.

13. For that matter, Nietzsche considers Arabs and Hebrews to be among the "strong races" (unpublished fragment 11 [287], November 1887–March 1888), meaning, on the one hand, that these cultural communities are not subsumed under the notion of "Semites," and on the other hand, that the distinction between communities has to do with other than "racial" criteria.

14. See Maurice Olender, *Race and Erudition*, as well as Léon Poliakov, *The Aryan Myth*, trans. Edmund Howard (New York: Basic Books, 1974), 300: "The 'blond beast' and the 'master race' are not the only Nietzschean slogans which, taken out of context, can be fitted into racist catechisms. By the way, some of the veteran anti-Semites were not in the least deceived. Eugen Dühring insinuated that Nietzsche was a Jew, and Theodor Fritsch warned youthful students against this 'insolent Pole.'"

15. Regarding the Dorians, who had a less sophisticated culture than that of the future Attica, Nietzsche was thinking of Karl Otfried Müller's *Die Dorier* (1824), if only because Müller was a follower of Böckh, like Nietzsche himself, as

unquestionably illustrated by his course "The Encyclopedia of Classical Philology" (1873–74). See, on these questions, William M. Calder III and Renate Schlesier, eds., *Zwischen Rationalismus und Romantik: Karl Otfried Müller und die antike Kultur* (Darmstadt, 1998).

16. Nietzsche, *On the Genealogy of Morals*, 42, I, §11.

17. Alexandre Koyré, *The Astronomic Revolution*, trans. R. E. W. Maddison (London: Routledge, 2009 [1973]), 77. Translation modified.

18. J. T. Clark, "The Philosophy of Science and History of Science," *Critical Problems in the History of Science* (Madison: University of Wisconsin Press, 1962), 103.

19. Georges Canguilhem, *Études d'histoire et de philosophie des sciences* (Paris: Vrin, 1983), 21ff.

20. Moreover, it would be too simple and less unsettling to consider Bäumler a mere Nazi idealogue. We must also take into account that he was, as we have noted, a brilliant commentator on Kant. While it is banal to dig up the contradictory attitudes of revolutionary periods, we must constantly bear in mind the effective perversion at work here, which is given free rein. There is no doubt of Bäumler's anti-Semitism, but his involvement with the Nazis reveals what was in all probability also a mixture of socially ambitious opportunism and fascination with the violent exercise of power conflated with audacity and cowardly servitude. This well-educated, cultivated professor ends his first course at the University of Berlin on May 10, 1933, by proclaiming: "We can say what national socialism means within the order of spirit in a single phrase: replacing the educated man with the soldier." And the procession of SA soldiers who had been in this course proceeded to burn books at Bebelplatz. Bäumler (who died at the age of eighty-eight in 1968, after two years of imprisonment in 1945, and who never returned to teaching) gave his full consent here, convinced that this would result in the purging of what he rejected as "the poison that has accumulated as the result of deceitful tolerance, and which we will do away with today."

21. Nietzsche, *The Antichrist*, §1, in Friedrich Nietzsche, *The Anti-Christ, Ecce Homo, Twilight of the Idols, and Other Writings*, ed. Aaron Ridley and Judith Norman, trans. Judith Norman (Cambridge: Cambridge University Press, 2005), 3.

22. *Histories*, IV, 14. On the group of philosophers called the "Hyperboreans" or "Apollonians," see Giorgio Colli, *La Sapienza greca*, vol. 1 (Milan: Adelphi, 1990).

23. Pindar, *Olympian Odes*, III, 31–33, and *Pythian Odes*, X, 30–36. The Hyperboreans represent an "ironic golden age." Pindar was inspired by the myth of ages found in Hesiod's *Works and Days*, but with differences relating to existing rituals. The Hyperboreans are mortals who sacrifice asses (sacrifices are absent from the Hesiodic golden age, where gods and humans are closer). Asses, as usual, are lubricious. Apollo can contemplate their "trained *hubris*," while the golden age is a time of joy that, for Hesiod, serves as a reference to *dikè*, or justice, the opposite of *hubris*. Pindar relocates the myth of Perseus and the Gorgon (killed in Africa) to the golden age without explanation, thus introducing a semantic link between the joy of this place and petrification. The only mortal incursion—since no one but Perseus could have found the path—is destructive. Pindar makes clear

that this is an impracticable "idea," which brings about an image of divine and human joy: mortals sing and dance for the immediate pleasure of the god.

24. See Nietzsche, *Beyond Good and Evil*, §251. Friedrich Nietzsche, *Beyond Good and Evil*, trans. Walter Kaufmann (New York: Random House, 1966).

25. Bäumler, *Nietzsche, der Philosoph und Politiker*, 180–83.

26. See Nietzsche, *The Gay Science*, §§149, 350, 358. Friedrich Nietzsche, *The Gay Science*, trans. Walter Kaufmann (New York: Random House, 1974).

27. Nietzsche, "The Wanderer and His Shadow," §215, in Friedrich Nietzsche, *Human, All Too Human*, trans. R. J. Hollingdale (Cambridge: Cambridge University Press, 1996), 365.

Nietzsche under Nazism

1. It is important not to lose sight of the fact that Hitler himself did not expect much from the theoretical products of the ideologues who worked for him. Indeed, he said that he couldn't fully comprehend Alfred Rosenberg's *Myth of the 20ᵗʰ Century*. See Henry Picker, *Hitlers Tischgespräche im Führerhauptquartier 1941–1942* (Stuttgart: Seewald Verlag, 1963), 270. Moreover, Rosenberg's book was far from receiving unanimous acclaim in the Nazi party as well among peripheral "fellow travelers."

2. It's very likely that Lang himself invented this anecdote, for even if he was approached by Goebbels's agents, it is doubtful that he ever met the man personally. See Patrick McGilligan, *Fritz Lang: The Nature of the Beast* (Minneapolis: University of Minnesota Press, 1997).

3. In the fields of scientific knowledge and philosophy, such a rejection of the difference between properly hypothetical registers and fields of application leads to holding "method" at bay. Method is immediately placed under suspicion once it doesn't function (and this is another naivety) as an instrument pure and simple, a go-between of the *interpretandum* and the *interpretandi*, to such a degree that it is rejected altogether, on the grounds that mediation affects the rise of ideas and imposes falsifying meanderings on their fall that slow down the dynamic of their authentic trajectory.

4. Martha Zapata Galindo, in her book *Triumph des Willens zur Macht* (Hamburg: Argument, 1995) as well as in her contribution to the volume edited by Sandro Barbera and Renate Müller-Buck, *Nietzsche nach dem Ersten Weltkrieg* (vol. 1, [Pisa: ETS, 2006], 167–98, in particular, 184–96), takes stock of the use of Nietzsche's texts in various sectors where Nazi ideology was deployed. She underlines the fact that there was never a consensus about Nietzsche within the Nazi faction, and that no official "portrait" of him was created. Each ideologue carefully selected whatever would allow him to claim Nietzsche's authority while avoiding anything that could refute such capture.

5. Hans Blumenberg, *Begriffe in Geschichten* (Frankfurt am Main: Suhrkamp, 1998), 72.

6. Adolf Hitler, *Mein Kampf*, trans. James Murphy (Project Gutenberg of Australia, 2002), vol. 1, chap. 11. Nietzsche always rejected such positions: the end goal of the "will to power" is by no means the conservation of any "race" any more than it is the conservation of the human species.

7. On February 15, 1945, in an interview recorded by Martin Bormann, Hitler repeats: "I could not ignore the Jews as they sent the world into war once again, and they would not be saved this time, the vermin had to be expelled from Europe." On April 2, 1945, Hitler reinforced the idea of his historical role as primarily racist: "Nazism will be eternally recognized for having wiped out all the Jews from Germany and Central Europe." The day before his death, on April 29, he wrote, at the end of his last will and testament: "Above all I obligate the leadership of the nation and its followers to the most minute observation of the racial laws and to pitiless resistance against the universal poisoner of all people, international Judaism."

8. Hitler, *Mein Kampf*, vol. 1, chap. 4.

9. Hitler, *Mein Kampf*, vol. 2, chap. 1.

10. Nietzsche, *On the Genealogy of Morals*, 44, I, §12.

11. Nietzsche, *On the Genealogy of Morals*, 43, I, §12.

The Nietzsche Archives and the Reich

1. David Marc Hoffmann, *Zur Geschichte des Nietzsche-Archivs* (Berlin: De Gruyter, 1991).

2. This edition, called the *Grossoktavausgabe*, was published in nineteen volumes between 1894 and 1913, by Naumann in Leipzig and later by Kröner.

3. Elisabeth Förster-Nietzsche had taken up the habit of gathering excerpts of her brother's work and signing them. Among many examples, we will just mention the collection *Paroles prophétiques sur les États et les peuples* (Leipzig: Kröner, 1924), which compiles quotations from Nietzsche targeting the state and republican, democratic, and socialist ideals—that is, the Weimar Republic.

4. Elisabeth Förster-Nietzsche wasted no time in writing him a letter, in which she said: "I have been informed that you have adopted an attitude of strict rejection regarding the 3rd Reich and its Führer, and your departure from the Archives, which display a deep respect for him, seems to go hand in hand with this attitude. [. . .] But perhaps I am mistaken and there are other reasons for your departure than our adherence to the ideals of national socialism." Oswald Spengler, *Briefe* (Munich: Beck, 1963, 749). The reason Spengler gives is clearly an entirely different one: "I firmly disagree with the positions advanced in Oehler's book [*Friedrich Nietzsche und die deutsche Zukunft* (Leipzig: Armanen, 1935)]. We are concerned either with Nietzsche's philosophy or with that of the Archives, and when the two are in contradiction, it is necessary to choose a side" (Spengler, *Briefe*, 751).

5. By 1945, five volumes of Nietzsche's works and four of his correspondence would be published. After 1945, the editions would not continue. The minister of education and justice of Thuringia also supported the work of the Nietzsche Archives.

6. See David Marc Hoffmann, *Zur Geschichte des Nietzsche-Archivs*, 332–35. Another, more complete edition would come out from Bong & Co in Leipzig.

7. Walter Benjamin, *Gesammelte Schriften*, vol. 3 (Frankfurt am Main: Suhrkamp, 1972), 323–26.

8. Nietzsche, *Beyond Good and Evil*, 186, §251.

9. Nietzsche, *Beyond Good and Evil*, 187.

10. Erich Podach, *The Madness of Nietzsche*, trans. F. A. Voigt (London: Putnam, 1931).

11. Beyond the fact that Carl August Emge (1886–1970) was the director of the Archives for a time, he was the only holder of a chair in philosophy of law in Germany during the Nazi period. After 1949, he held a seat at the Mainz Academy of Science and Literature and was even, from 1953 on, part of a commission of inquiry on refugees (!) in the context of European institutions.

12. Report of the 8th meeting of the *Gesellschaft der Freunde des Nietzsche-Archivs*, December 6, 1933.

13. This issue can now be read in its entirety in the French original online at http://i.a.m.free.fr/acephale/revue.html. All issues of the review were published by Jean-Michel Place, Paris, 1995. The betrayals and distortions of Nietzsche's work are clearly delineated in this issue. Even the more "scholarly" interpretive diversions, such as those of Bäumler, are exposed, as are the many and various manipulations to which his writings gave rise.

14. Georges Bataille, "Nietzsche and the Fascists," in *Visions of Excess: Selected Writings (1927–1939)*, trans. Allan Stoekl (Minneapolis: University of Minnesota Press, 1985), 185. Trans. modified.

15. See *Nietzsche-Studien* 18 (1989): 40 ff.

The Will to Power: An Editorial Fiction

1. Nietzsche, *The Gay Science*, 86.

2. Nietzsche, *Thus Spoke Zarathustra*, I, 42; Friedrich Nietzsche, *Thus Spoke Zarathustra*, ed. Adrian del Caro and Robert B. Pippin, trans. Adrian del Caro (Cambridge: Cambridge University Press, 2006).

3. Thanks to the immense philological work Giorgio Colli and Mazzino Montinari have carried out from the 1960s on, both for the complete edition of Nietzsche's work in Italian published by Einaudi and for the German by de Gruyter, the unpublished fragments have been put in chronological order. The first number cited refers to the part of a journal, notebook, or collection of papers that Nietzsche used during a given period, and the number in brackets indicates the order of this fragment in this part of the journal. The fragment can thus easily be identified in any edition, whether it be German, Italian, French, or English, provided it follows the chronology established by Colli and Montinari. The entirety of this edition in German is accessible at the site www.Nietzschesource.org. [There is not yet a full translation of Nietzsche's unpublished fragments in English. The project of their translation and publication is underway from Stanford University Press, who are putting out the first English-language edition of Nietzsche's complete works. Where English translations of the unpublished fragments are available from the Stanford editions, I have included, and cited, the official translations. Where no English translation exists, I have translated the fragments myself with reference to the online German edition cited above.—Translator]

4. Nietzsche, fragment 5 [1] 1, November 1882–February 1883, Friedrich Nietzsche, *Unpublished Fragments from the Period of* Thus Spoke Zarathustra *(Summer 1882–Winter 1883/1884)*, *The Complete Works of Friedrich Nietzsche*,

vol. 14, trans. Paul S. Loeb and David F. Tinsley (Stanford: Stanford University Press, 2019), 166. At the start of 1887, Nietzsche repeats this, affirming his "new definition of the concept of 'life' as will to power" (7 [54], end of 1886–spring 1887).

5. Nietzsche, *Thus Spoke Zarathustra*, II, 88–89.

6. Friedrich Nietzsche, *Unpublished Fragments (Spring 1885–Spring 1886)*, *The Complete Works of Friedrich Nietzsche*, vol. 16, trans. Adrian del Caro (Stanford: Stanford University Press, 2019), 99.

7. Nietzsche, *Unpublished Fragments (Spring 1885–Spring 1886)*, 84.

8. Nietzsche, *Unpublished Fragments (Spring 1885–Spring 1886)*, 106–7.

9. Nietzsche, *Unpublished Fragments (Spring 1885–Spring 1886)*, 168–69.

10. Nietzsche, *Unpublished Fragments (Spring 1885–Spring 1886)*, 176.

11. Nietzsche, *Unpublished Fragments (Spring 1885–Spring 1886)*, 179–80.

12. Nietzsche, *Beyond Good and Evil*, 26.

13. Nietzsche, *Unpublished Fragments (Spring 1885–Spring 1886)*, 182.

14. Nietzsche, *Unpublished Fragments (Spring 1885–Spring 1886)*, 207.

15. Nietzsche, *Unpublished Fragments (Spring 1885–Spring 1886)*, 214.

16. Nietzsche, *Unpublished Fragments (Spring 1885–Spring 1886)*, 208.

17. Nietzsche, *Unpublished Fragments (Spring 1885–Spring 1886)*, 337.

18. Nietzsche, *Unpublished Fragments (Spring 1885–Spring 1886)*, 350. Trans. mod.

19. See for example Nietzsche, fragment 2 [131], autumn 1885–autumn 1886, Nietzsche, *Unpublished Fragments (Spring 1885–Spring 1886)*, 367ff.

20. This is fragment 19 [4], where Nietzsche plans out a twelve-chapter book. This outline corresponds to existing and contemporary manuscripts, namely *Twilight of the Idols* and *The Antichrist*.

21. Nietzsche, *Twilight of the Idols*, trans. Richard Polt (Cambridge, MA: Hackett, 1997), 4. Trans. mod.

22. See Mazzino Montinari's patient deconstruction of the attempts to produce a book called "The Will to Power" in *Nietzsche lesen* (Berlin: De Gruyter, 1982).

The "Will to Power": A Concept

1. Friedrich Nietzsche, *Unpublished Fragments from the Period of* Human, All Too Human I *(Winter 1874/75–Winter 1877/78)*, *The Complete Works of Friedrich Nietzsche*, vol. 12, trans. Gary Handwerk (Stanford: Stanford University Press, 2021), 386.

2. Nietzsche, *Ecce Homo*, "Nietzsche's Preface," §4; Friedrich Nietzsche, *On the Genealogy of Morals* and *Ecce Homo*, ed. and trans. Walter Kaufmann (New York: Vintage, 1967), 219.

3. Nietzsche, "Why I Write Such Good Books," "*The Birth of Tragedy*," *Ecce Homo*, 275, §4.

4. Nietzsche, "Why I Am a Destiny," *Ecce Homo*, 329, §4.

5. Nietzsche, "On Old and New Tablets," *Zarathustra*, 171, III, §26.

6. Nietzsche, "Why I Write Such Good Books," "*Thus Spoke Zarathustra*," *Ecce Homo*, 295, §1. Trans. mod.

7. Nietzsche, "Why I Write Such Good Books," "*Thus Spoke Zarathustra*," *Ecce Homo*, 296, §1.

8. Nietzsche, "Why I Write Such Good Books," "*Thus Spoke Zarathustra*," *Ecce Homo*, 306, §6.

9. Nietzsche, "On Redemption," *Zarathustra*, II, 110. Trans. mod.

10. Nietzsche, "Why I Write Such Good Books," "*Beyond Good and Evil*," *Ecce Homo*, 310, §1.

11. Nietzsche, "Why I Write Such Good Books," "*Beyond Good and Evil*," *Ecce Homo*, 310, §1.

12. Nietzsche, "Why I Write Such Good Books," "*Genealogy of Morals*," *Ecce Homo*, 313.

13. Nietzsche to Karl Knortz, June 21, 1888, The Nietzsche Channel. http://www.theNietzschechannel.com/. Trans. mod.

14. Nietzsche to Georg Brandes, December 2, 1887, The Nietzsche Channel, trans. mod.

15. Nietzsche, *The Gay Science*, 343, §381.

16. Nietzsche, *Beyond Good and Evil*, 27, §39.

17. Nietzsche, *Beyond Good and Evil*, 30, §42.

18. Nietzsche, *Beyond Good and Evil*, 289, §229.

19. Nietzsche, fragment 5 [9], 1886.

20. Nietzsche to Georg Brandes, December 2, 1887. The Nietzsche Channel.

21. This is clearly not the case. In her book *Hitler et les races: L'anthropologie national-socialiste* (Paris: Berg International, 2013), Anne Quinchon-Caudal discusses Nietzsche's case (p. 22).

22. Nietzsche, *Beyond Good and Evil*, 156, §227.

23. Nietzsche, *Beyond Good and Evil*, 156, §227.

24. Nietzsche, *Thus Spoke Zarathustra*, II, 88.

25. Nietzsche, *Beyond Good and Evil*, 31, §23.

26. Nietzsche, *Beyond Good and Evil*, 16, §9.

27. Nietzsche, *Ecce Homo*, "Why I Write Such Good Books," 261, §1.

28. Nietzsche, *Beyond Good and Evil*, 21, §13.

29. Nietzsche, *Beyond Good and Evil*, 21, §22.

30. Nietzsche, "Morality as Anti-Nature," *Twilight of the Idols*, 25, §1. In paragraph 3, he writes: "The spiritualization of sensuality is known as *love*" and, in the same place: "Another triumph is our spiritualization of *enmity*. It consists in a deep grasp of the value of having enemies" (*Twilight of the Idols*, 26, §3).

31. Nietzsche, *Beyond Good and Evil*, §22.

32. Nietzsche, *Beyond Good and Evil*, §230.

33. Nietzsche, *Beyond Good and Evil*, 30, §22. Trans. mod.

34. Nietzsche, *Beyond Good and Evil*, 30, §22.

35. Nietzsche, *Beyond Good and Evil*, 136, §211.

36. Nietzsche, *Beyond Good and Evil*, 136, §259.

37. Nietzsche, *Beyond Good and Evil*, 155–56, §227.

38. Nietzsche, *Beyond Good and Evil*, 48, §36.

39. Nietzsche, *Beyond Good and Evil*, 48, §36, Trans. mod.

40. Nietzsche, *Beyond Good and Evil*, 47, §36.

41. Nietzsche, *Beyond Good and Evil*, 47–48.

The Overman

1. Nietzsche, *On the Genealogy of Morals*, 43, I, §11.

2. Nietzsche, *On the Genealogy of Morals*, 44, I, §12.

3. Nietzsche, *Beyond Good and Evil*, 74, §62.

4. Nietzsche, *Thus Spoke Zarathustra*, "On Old and New Tablets," 158, III, §3.

5. Nietzsche, fragment 3 [1], 385 and 386, summer–autumn 1882, *Unpublished Fragments from the Period of* Thus Spoke Zarathustra *(Summer 1882– Winter 1883/1884)*, 86. Trans. mod. The fact that the overman is connected to reflections on compassion is in no way surprising: "The danger for the overman is compassion" (13 [1], Summer 1883, 396, trans. mod.). [Note: the recent English translation of the fragments from the period of *Zarathustra* translates "Übermensch" as "superhuman" and frequently pluralizes the term—with respect and honor to this translation decision, I have retranslated the term "Übermensch" as "overman" in keeping with de Launay's work and the tradition of Nietzschean terminology in English.—Translator]

6. Nietzsche, fragment 4 [116], November 1882–February 1883, *Unpublished Fragments from the Period of* Thus Spoke Zarathustra *(Summer 1882–Winter 1883/1884)*, 130. Trans. mod.

7. Nietzsche, fragment 4 [224], November 1882–February 1883, *Unpublished Fragments from the Period of* Thus Spoke Zarathustra *(Summer 1882–Winter 1883/1884)*, 153. Trans. mod.

8. Nietzsche, fragment 4 [84], November 1882–February 1883, *Unpublished Fragments from the Period of* Thus Spoke Zarathustra *(Summer 1882–Winter 1883/1884)*, 121. Trans. mod. See also 4 [110], from the same period: "Finally, I came to love the overman—since then I have *tolerated* humans. I want to bring them a new hope! And a new fear—said Zarathustra" (ibid., 129, trans. mod.).

9. Nietzsche, fragment 4 [181], November 1882–February 1883, *Unpublished Fragments from the Period of* Thus Spoke Zarathustra *(Summer 1882–Winter 1883/1884)*, 144. Trans. mod.

10. Nietzsche, fragment 5 [1], 270, November 1882–February 1883, *Unpublished Fragments from the Period of* Thus Spoke Zarathustra *(Summer 1882–Winter 1883/1884)*, 196.

11. Nietzsche, "Zarathustra's Prologue," *Thus Spoke Zarathustra*, 6, §3.

12. Nietzsche, "Zarathustra's Prologue," *Thus Spoke Zarathustra*, 7, §4.

13. Nietzsche, "Zarathustra's Prologue," *Thus Spoke Zarathustra*, 8, §4. *Zarathustra*, III, 3: "human being is a bridge and not an end"—it "must be overcome," 158. By the same token, in "On the Higher Man" (IV, 3), he writes: "what I am able to love in human beings is that they are a going over and a going under," 233.

14. Nietzsche, *On the Genealogy of Morals*, 96, II, §24. First emphasis added.

15. Nietzsche, "Why I Write Such Good Books," "Beyond Good and Evil," *Ecce Homo*, I, 310. Cf. the letter of October 4, 1884, to Overbeck: "To put it briefly, I must find disciples within my lifetime. And if my previous books do not play the role of fish hooks, they have 'missed their vocation.'" This recalls section 9 of the prologue to *Thus Spoke Zarathustra*: "let Zarathustra speak not to the people, but instead to companions! Zarathustra should not become the shepherd

and dog of a herd! To lure many away from the herd—for that I came" (*Zarathu-stra*, 14).

16. Nietzsche, "On Bestowing Virtue," *Thus Spoke Zarathustra*, 58, I, §2.

17. Nietzsche, "Why I Am a Destiny," *Ecce Homo*, 327, §1: "It is only begin-ning with me that the earth knows *great politics*."

18. Nietzsche, *On the Genealogy of Morals*, III, §9.

19. Nietzsche, fragment 4 [20], November 1882–February 1883, *Unpub-lished Fragments from the Period of* Thus Spoke Zarathustra *(Summer 1882–Winter 1883/1884)*, 98. Aphorism 109 of *The Gay Science* is just as clear: "The total character of the world, however, is in all eternity chaos—in the sense not of a lack of necessity by of a lack of order [. . .]. Let us beware of saying that there are laws in nature. There are only necessities [. . .]. Once you know that there are no purposes, you also know that there is no accident; for it is only beside a world of purposes that the word 'accident' has meaning" (§168).

20. Nietzsche, *Beyond Good and Evil*, 30–31, §22.

21. Nietzsche, *Beyond Good and Evil*, 30–31, §30.

22. Nietzsche, fragment 4 [75], November 1882–February 1883, *Unpub-lished Fragments from the Period of* Thus Spoke Zarathustra *(Summer 1882–Winter 1883/1884)*, 117.

23. Nietzsche, fragment 12 [43], Summer 1883, *Unpublished Fragments from the Period of* Thus Spoke Zarathustra *(Summer 1882–Winter 1883/1884)*, 367.

24. Nietzsche, "On the Blessed Isles," *Zarathustra*, 65.

25. Nietzsche, fragment 4 [171], November 1882–February 1883, *Unpub-lished Fragments from the Period of* Thus Spoke Zarathustra *(Summer 1882–Winter 1883/1884)*, 142. Trans. mod.

26. Cf. Fragments 10 [37] and 10 [41] of June–July 1883, and 13 [26] of Summer 1883, as well as "On Priests," *Zarathustra*, II.

27. Nietzsche, *On the Genealogy of Morals*, 54, I, 16. Cf. *The Gay Science*, V, 382. We should also be wary of the evocation of Cesare Borgia as "a sort of *overman* [. . .] in comparison to us." Cf. "Raids of an Untimely Man," *Twilight of the Idols*, 72, §37. Cf. as well Nietzsche's letter to Malwida von Meysenbug of October 20, 1888: "The overman for me is a hundred times more like Cesare Borgia than Christ."

28. Cf. Epicurus, "Letter to Menoeceus," 123: "For gods do exist, since we have clear knowledge of them. But they are not such as the many believe them to be. For they do not adhere to their own views about the gods. The man who denies the gods of the many is not impious, but rather he who ascribes to the gods the opinions of the many." The fact remains that, for Epicurus, the gods are unchanging and indifferent to us; they are in an eternal state of beatitude. Epicu-rus's mission was to persuade his fellow humans that they could also experience divine *eudemonia*, even if only at their own, inferior, level.

29. Nietzsche, *Beyond Good and Evil*, §62.

30. Nietzsche, "Why I Write Such Good Books," *Ecce Homo*, 261, §1.

31. Nietzsche, "Why I Write Such Good Books," "Thus Spoke Zarathustra," *Ecce Homo*, 305, §6.

32. Nietzsche, "Why I Am a Destiny," *Ecce Homo*, 331, §5.

33. Nietzsche, *Zarathustra*, III, 12, 3, 158–59.

34. Nietzsche, fragment 10 [47], June–July 1883, 337.

35. Nietzsche, fragment 35 [73], May–July 1885.

36. Nietzsche, fragment 27 [23], summer–autumn 1884, *Unpublished Fragments from the Period of* Thus Spoke Zarathustra *(Spring 1884–Winter 1884/85)*, 261.

37. Nietzsche, fragment 11 [413], November 1887–March 1888. This fragment is contemporaneous with *On the Genealogy of Morals* and with Nietzsche's last writings on the themes surrounding the concept of the "will to power."

38. That is, what Nietzsche calls the "basic text of *homo natura*" (Nietzsche, *Beyond Good and Evil*, §230, 161).

39. Nietzsche, *Beyond Good and Evil*, 43, §30.

40. In Greek in the text.

41. Nietzsche, *Beyond Good and Evil*, 72, §61: "The philosopher as *we* understand him, we free spirits—as the man of the most comprehensive responsibility who has the conscience for the over-all development of man," as well as *On the Genealogy of Morals*, 56, I, §17: "*All* the sciences have from now on to prepare the way for the future task of the philosophers: this task understood as the solution to the *problem of value*, the determination of the *order of rank among values*."

42. Hans Blumenberg understands this perfectly: "To give oneself the history that sets one free of history, or that only endorses what is present without putting it in question, would have meant, so to speak, to secede from history and throw off its burden." *The Legitimacy of the Modern Age*, trans. Robert M. Wallace (Cambridge: MIT Press, 1999), 143. However, the overman cannot be considered the height of self-affirmation proper to the "modern age," for despite this appearance, he remains within a kind of desperate self-affirmation at the very moment when Nietzsche reminds us that the individual is never anything more than a "slice of fate" (*Twilight of the Idols*, "Morality as Anti-Nature," 29, §6) and that humanity is, in all likelihood, destined to disappear (cf. the opening of "On Truth and Lie in an Extra-moral Sense"). In the conclusion of his chapter devoted to the characterization of the "modern age," Blumenberg quotes a passage from *Dialogues on the Commerce in Wheat* by Ferdinando Galiani, of whom Nietzsche was a great admirer. This passage may indeed help us to understand the origins of the metaphor of the overman: "We are too small. For nature, space, motion are nothing, but we cannot wait" (*Legitimacy of the Modern Age*, 226).

43. Nietzsche, *Beyond Good and Evil*, 15–16, §9.

44. Nietzsche, *Beyond Good and Evil*, 16.

45. Nietzsche, *Beyond Good and Evil*, 15, §8. The ancient mystery Nietzsche invokes here is not Greek; it is distantly inspired by the Roman Saturnalia, but it is in fact the festival of the ass—referring to the ass that Mary rode during the flight into Egypt, or the one that carried Jesus into Jerusalem—also known as the festival of fools. The Latin quotation originates from the farcical song sung during these festivals, translating to: "The ass arrived, beautiful and most brave" (trans. Walter Kaufmann in *Beyond Good and Evil*, 15).

Darwinism?

1. Nietzsche, fragment 11 [413], November 1887–March 1888.

2. Nietzsche, fragment 19 [87]. At Basel, Nietzsche worked on the subject of teleology "from Kant to Darwin" in the context of discussions on the existence or

nonexistence of an "intelligent plan" at work in nature. Darwin evidently offered a rational basis for the critique of providentialism. See Gilbert Merlio's article, "Nietzsche, Darwin et le darwinisme," *Revue germanique international* 10 (2009): 125–45.

3. Nietzsche, fragment 19 [132].

4. Nietzsche, fragment 27 [17], spring–autumn 1873.

5. Nietzsche, fragment 12 [22], summer–September 1875, *Unpublished Fragments from the Period of* Human, All Too Human I *(Winter 1874/75–Winter 1877/78)*, 229.

6. Charles Darwin, *On the Origin of Species* (New York: D. Appleton, 1861), 84. On the misunderstandings and misinterpretations in the reception of Darwin by racist ideologues who essentially transposed what he says about breeding practices onto the evolution of the human species, see Michele Cammelli, "La question de la 'race' entre science et élevage," *Failles* 2 (2006): 188–205.

7. Darwin, *On the Origin of Species*, 87.

8. Nietzsche, fragment 10 [B42], spring 1880–spring 1881.

9. Nietzsche, *Dawn*, §453; Friedrich Nietzsche, *Dawn: The Complete Works of Friedrich Nietzsche*, vol. 5, trans. Britain Smith (Stanford: Stanford University Press, 2011), 232.

10. See also *Beyond Good and Evil*, §210.

11. Nietzsche, fragment 7 [261], spring–summer 1883.

12. Nietzsche, fragment 24 [1], October–November 1888.

13. Nietzsche, fragment 25 [7], December 1888–January 1889. We may be tempted to detect a Nietzschean echo in the work of Peter Altenberg, that turn-of-the-century figure who, in 1906, writes the following about individuality in *Prodromos*: "To the extent that an individuality has any reason for being, if only the appearance of a reason, it can only be a prototype, an anticipated thing within the organic evolution of the human in general." *Ausgewählte Werke*, vol. 1 (Munich: Hanser, 1979), 129.

14. Nietzsche, fragment 11 [177], spring–autumn 1881: "Darwin's assertions need to be proven—through trials! The same is true of the emergence of superior organisms from inferior ones. Many trials were needed over millennia! Educating monkeys to make them into men."

15. Nietzsche, fragment 28 [45], autumn 1884, *Unpublished Fragments from the Period of* Thus Spoke Zarathustra *(Spring 1884–Winter 1884/85)*, 293–94. See Nietzsche, *Beyond Good and Evil*, §14, and *The Gay Science*, 349: "The whole of English Darwinism breathes something like the musty air of English overpopulation, like the smell of the distress and overcrowding of small people" (*The Gay Science*, 349, 292).

16. Nietzsche, fragment 34 [73], April–June 1885, *Unpublished Fragments (Spring 1885–Spring 1886)*, 18. See also *The Gay Science*, §357: "without Hegel there could have been no Darwin" (*The Gay Science*, 305). It goes without saying, regarding Lamarck, that for Nietzsche it is not a question of the heredity of "acquired characters": on the one hand, because evolution is constant and does not necessarily build or accumulate in the sense of one form of progress or another. And, on the other hand, importantly, because everything that is temporarily "inherited" is simply imposed at the end of a struggle between drives, and what

"prevails" does so only for a limited time. Regarding Hegel, and in terms of a theory of history, "syntheses" are nothing other than very temporary compromises.

17. Nietzsche, fragment 11 [106], spring–autumn 1881: "'Useful-harmful!' 'Utilitarian!' The presupposition of such talk is that the direction of human (or animal or plant) evolution *has already been decided.* As if thousands of evolutions weren't possible at every point!"

18. Nietzsche, fragment 11 [106], spring–autumn 1881

19. Nietzsche, fragment 15 [120], spring 1888.

20. This is a quotation from a hymn of Luther's.

21. Nietzsche, "Raids of an Untimely Man," *Twilight of the Idols*, 59, §14. Fragment 14 [133].

22. Georges Canguilhem, *Knowledge of Life*, trans. Stefanos Geroulanos and Daniela Ginsburg (New York: Fordham University Press, 2008), xx.

23. We need only think of Ernst Haeckel, who was one of the first scientists to understand psychology as a branch of physiology. Nietzsche was directly inspired by this (see the first chapter of *Human, All Too Human*), although he opposes Haeckel's confidence in the constant progress of human evolution in the most decisive terms. Haeckel was also used in part by the Nazis, who exploited his eugenicist vision as well as his conceptions of the hygiene of the race, while banning the monist union he had founded at the university, which they considered a ferment of intellectual resistance owing to its rationalist and, in spite of everything, scientific independence.

24. Nietzsche, fragment 7 [9], end of 1886–spring 1887: "Life is *not* the adaptation of internal conditions to external conditions, but will to power, which, from within, continually subjects and incorporates more from the 'outside.'" In the same fragment, Nietzsche denounces the "fundamental errors of contemporary biologists" who believe in the conservation of the species while surreptitiously reinstating "the superior value of altruism in itself." The individual is interested not in the species but in its greatest externalization of power.

25. Nietzsche, *The Gay Science*, 177, §121.

26. Nietzsche, fragment 11 [122], spring–autumn 1881: "The entirety of animal and human drives lasted an endless time [. . .], it would be impossible to eradicate these drives for the individual—he consists of them [. . .]. The conflict between these drives is as necessary as any struggle, for suffering does not influence the species more than the death of individuals."

27. Nietzsche, fragment 11 [84], spring–autumn 1881: "Our entire world is merely the *ash* of numberless *living* beings: and even if the living is so small in comparison to the whole, it is true that *everything* has been transformed into life, and so it goes on. Let us say that there is an eternal duration, and therefore an eternal metabolism."

Eternal Return

1. Nietzsche, "Assorted Opinions and Maxims," *Human, All Too Human*, 243, §128.

2. Nietzsche, "Why I Write Such Good Books," "Beyond Good and Evil," *Ecce Homo*.

3. Nietzsche, "Why I Am So Clever," *Ecce Homo*, 251, §7.

4. Nietzsche, fragment 16 [49], autumn 1883, *Unpublished Fragments from the Period of* Thus Spoke Zarathustra *(Summer 1882–Winter 1883/1884)*, 464. Trans. mod.

5. Nietzsche, fragment 20 [2], August 1883, *Unpublished Fragments from the Period of* Thus Spoke Zarathustra *(Summer 1882–Winter 1883/1884)*, 532. See also *Human, All Too Human*, I, §33, where Nietzsche already outlined his conception in speaking of a cyclic dynamic of cultures (247, 249, 251).

6. Nietzsche, fragment 11 [141], spring–autumn 1881. "The greatest weight" is the title of aphorism 341 of *The Gay Science*, which is the first occurrence of the phrase "eternal return" in his published works.

7. Lou Andreas-Salomé, *Nietzsche*, trans. Siegfried Mandel (Chicago: University of Illinois Press, 2001).

8. Or, if you prefer, Deuteronomy 19:15.

9. Nietzsche, "The Convalescent," *Zarathustra*, III, §2.

10. Georg Simmel, *Schopenhauer und Nietzsche* (Leipzig, 1907), 254.

11. See, among other passages, fragments 26 [374], 26 [432], 27 [27], summer–autumn 1884, and 37 [4], June–July 1885: "Using the body as a guide, as I mentioned, we learn that our life is only possible through the interplay of many intelligences of very unequal value and therefore only through a constant thousand-fold obeying and commanding—morally spoken: through the incessant exercise of many *virtues*." Nietzsche, *Unpublished Fragments (Spring 1885–Spring 1886)*, 141.

12. Nietzsche, "Why I Write Such Good Books," *Ecce Homo*, §3.

13. Plato, *Timaeus*, 39d.

14. Nietzsche, *The Gay Science*, 237, §341.

15. Nietzsche, "The Convalescent," *Zarathustra*, 177–78, III, §2. Trans. mod.

16. Nietzsche, "The Convalescent," *Zarathustra*, 178, III, §2. Trans. mod.

17. Nietzsche, "The Convalescent," *Zarathustra*, 178–79, III, §2.

18. Nietzsche, *Ecce Homo*, "Why I Am So Wise," §3. This page has its own history; after writing it by hand, Nietzsche wanted to substitute a previous version with it—the version that was first printed in the 1908 edition and afterward, until Giorgio Colli and Mazzino Montinari's edition. The page is not included in Walter Kaufmann's English translation.

19. Nietzsche, *Human, All Too Human*, 12, §1.

20. Nietzsche, fragment 11 [148], spring–autumn 1881. In the summer of 1881, Nietzsche read Mayer's *Die Mechanik der Wärme* and drew from this text a justification for his hypothesis: the principle of the conservation of energy, for him, entails the eternal return (see 5 [54], spring 1886–autumn 1887).

21. Nietzsche, *Beyond Good and Evil*, 12. Nietzsche never changed his mind about this, from his first readings of Roger Joseph Boscovich in 1873 onward (see fragment 26 [12], spring 1873).

22. Nietzsche, fragment 11 [205], spring–autumn 1881.

23. Nietzsche, fragment 11 [157], spring–autumn 1881.

24. Nietzsche, fragment 11 [202], spring–autumn 1881.

25. Nietzsche, fragment 11 [141], spring–autumn 1881.

26. Nietzsche, "What I Owe to the Ancients," *Twilight of the Idols*, 87, §2.

27. Nietzsche, "What I Owe to the Ancients," *Twilight of the Idols*, 90, §4. Trans. mod.

28. Nietzsche, "What I Owe to the Ancients," *Twilight of the Idols*, 91, §5. Trans. mod.

29. Nietzsche, "Why I Write Such Good Books," *Ecce Homo*, 306, §6.

30. Nietzsche, fragment 13 [1], summer 1883.

31. Nietzsche, *Human, All Too Human*, 74, §138.

32. Nietzsche, "Why I Write Such Good Books," "*Thus Spoke Zarathustra*," *Ecce Homo*, 295, §1.

33. Nietzsche self-published this fourth part in an edition of fifty copies which he later attempted to recuperate so as to keep others from reading it (cf. for example, the letter to his sister of May 22, 1885).

34. Nietzsche, fragment 27 [80], summer–autumn 1884, *Unpublished Fragments from the Period of* Thus Spoke Zarathustra *(Spring 1884–Winter 1884/85)*, 274. See also fragment 5 [70], 1887.

35. Nietzsche, fragment 10 [47], June–July 1883; 16 [54], autumn 1883.

36. See for example Nietzsche, fragments 2 [74]; 5 [75], autumn 1885–autumn 1886; 6 [26], summer 1887–spring 1887; 12 [2], beginning of 1888; 16 [71] and 16 [72], spring–summer 1888; 18 [17], August 1888.

37. Nietzsche, *Beyond Good and Evil*, 68, §56.

38. Nietzsche, *Beyond Good and Evil*, 53, §43. These words are put in the mouth of the "philosopher[s] of the future," the "coming philosophers." The following aphorism indicates the direct identification of these figures with Nietzsche himself.

39. See for example Nietzsche, fragments 24 [4], winter 1883–1884; 25 [1], spring 1884; 25 [323], spring 1884.

40. Nietzsche, fragment 24 [4], winter 1883–1884, *Unpublished Fragments from the Period of* Thus Spoke Zarathustra *(Spring 1884–Winter 1884/85)*, 585.

41. Nietzsche, "Why I Am a Destiny," *Ecce Homo*, 333, §8. Trans. mod. It should not escape us that this phrase, "breaking humanity in two," was used close to two millennia earlier by certain Gnostics (particularly Basilides) to describe . . . Christ.

42. Nietzsche, "What I Owe to the Ancients," *Twilight of the Idols*, 91, §5.

43. Nietzsche, "What I Owe to the Ancients," *Twilight of the Idols*, 91, §5.

44. Nietzsche, fragment 5 [1], 1, autumn 1882: "Will to live? I have always only found will to power in its place." *Unpublished Fragments from the Period of* Thus Spoke Zarathustra *(Spring 1884–Winter 1884/85)*, 166.

45. See Nietzsche, "On Old and New Tablets," *Zarathustra*, III, §3; "Why I Am So Clever," *Ecce Homo*, §10.

46. Nietzsche, fragment 25 [7], December 1888–January 1998.

47. Nietzsche, "On Old and New Tablets," *Zarathustra*, III, 163, §12.

48. See Hans Jonas, "Gnosticism and Modern Nihilism," *Social Research* 19 (December 1952), as well as Eric Voegelin, *Science, Politics, and Gnosticism* (Wilmington, DE: ISI Books, 2004 [1958]).

49. Nietzsche, *The Anti-Christ*, in *The Anti-Christ, Ecce Homo, Twilight of the Idols, and Other Writings*, trans. Judith Norman (Cambridge: Cambridge University Press, 2005), 66.

29. This etymology is indeed viable, with *eurus* meaning "vast" or "ope[n]" *ôps* meaning "gaze" or "view." Herodotus, however, says that the origi[nal] name is unknown (*Histories* 4.45). There are, of course, many "E[…]" different ones for Hesiod, Homer, Pindar, etc.

30. Nietzsche, "The Wanderer and His Shadow," §[…] of Europe is irresistible" (*Human, All Too Human.* […]

31. Nietzsche, "The Wanderer and His S[hadow,"…] Ernst Troeltsch, *Der Historismus und sei[n…]* chaps. III/2 and III/3.

32. Nietzsche, "The Wand[erer…] *Human*, 365.

33. Nietzsche, "A[…] *Human*, 252.

34. Nie[…]

35[…]

H[…]

4[…]
45.[…]
46. N[…]
47. Nie[…] spirit will be a[…] the artist which […] the overman, who […] of fusion and overco[…] very idea of the eternal[…] to the temptation of a co[…] this would merely be a regr[…] Romanticism.

48. Nietzsche, *Human, All* […]

49. Heinrich von Treitschke, […] Are Our Misfortune" in Richard S. […] *Anthology of Texts* (Lexington, MA: D[…]

50. Treitschke, "Unsere Ansichten," […]

Wagner's 1969 work *Das Judenthum in der Musik* illuminating. Nietzsche takes up the patristic and scholastic use of the term "Jewish," meant to designate an attachment to the empirical and the literal. The "day when men shall be noble" is a quotation from memory (and incorrect) of Goethe's epilogue to Schiller's *Song of the Bell* (Goethe had spoken of a day "for the noble being").

9. Nietzsche to Siegfried Lipiner, August 24, 1877. The Nietzsche Channel.

10. Wagner, "Public and Popularity," in Richard Wagner, *Religion and Art,* trans. William Ashton Ellis (Lincoln: University of Nebraska Press, 1994), 57.

11. Catherine Alison Phillips, *Cosima Wagner* (New York: Knopf, 1931), 742.

12. Here is the text of that letter:

Herewith I am returning to you the three issues of *Correspondenz* [a well-known anti-Semitic journal], thanking you for permitting me to cast a glance at the muddle of principles that lie at the heart of this strange movement. Yet I ask you in the future not to provide me with these mailings: I fear, in the end, for my patience. Believe me: this abominable "wanting to have a say" of noisy dilettantes about the *value* of people and races, this subjection to "authorities" who are utterly rejected with cold contempt by every sensible mind (e.g., E. Dühring, R. Wagner, Ebrard, Wahrmund, P. de Lagarde—who among these in questions of morality and history is the most unqualified, the most unjust?), these constant, absurd falsifications and rationalizations of vague concepts, "Germanic," "Semitic," "Aryan," "Christian," "German"— of that could in the long run cause me to lose my temper and bring m[e…] the ironic benevolence with which I have hitherto observed the vi[…] velleities and pharisaisms of modern Germans.—And finally, how[…] think I feel when the name *Zarathustra* is mouthed by anti-Sem[…]

13. Bernhard Förster, March 29, 1887, The Nietzsche Ch[…] Nietzsche to Theodor Fritsch, a high school professor, was respons[…] large-scale anti-Semitic movement in the new Reich. On A[…] initiative, 267,000 signatures were collected and sent to B[…] restrict Jewish immigration, as well as demanding their en[…] and general education, as well as the ideas that Jesus was an Aryan, t[…] Förster upheld the ideas that Jesus was an Aryan, t[…] all societal ills, and that the German spirit was c[…] propaganda (*Antisemitische Correspondenz*), […] indignation, that his work was referenced[…] teacher, after publicly assaulting people[…] on the theme of Jesus as an Aryan, M[…] *Race, Religion, and Philology in the* […] (Cambridge: Harvard University[…]

14. See fragment 32 [32][…] Wagner if he does not give […]

15. Nietzsche declare[…] §251; fragments 12 [11][…] two categories: Jews […]

16. Nietzsche, […]

17. Nietzsch[…]

27. Nietzsche, "What I Owe to the Ancients," *Twilight of the Idols*, 90, §4. Trans. mod.

28. Nietzsche, "What I Owe to the Ancients," *Twilight of the Idols*, 91, §5. Trans. mod.

29. Nietzsche, "Why I Write Such Good Books," *Ecce Homo*, 306, §6.

30. Nietzsche, fragment 13 [1], summer 1883.

31. Nietzsche, *Human, All Too Human*, 74, §138.

32. Nietzsche, "Why I Write Such Good Books," *"Thus Spoke Zarathustra,"* *Ecce Homo*, 295, §1.

33. Nietzsche self-published this fourth part in an edition of fifty copies which he later attempted to recuperate so as to keep others from reading it (cf. for example, the letter to his sister of May 22, 1885).

34. Nietzsche, fragment 27 [80], summer–autumn 1884, *Unpublished Fragments from the Period of* Thus Spoke Zarathustra *(Spring 1884–Winter 1884/85)*, 274. See also fragment 5 [70], 1887.

35. Nietzsche, fragment 10 [47], June–July 1883; 16 [54], autumn 1883.

36. See for example Nietzsche, fragments 2 [74]; 5 [75], autumn 1885–autumn 1886; 6 [26], summer 1887–spring 1887; 12 [2], beginning of 1888; 16 [71] and 16 [72], spring–summer 1888; 18 [17], August 1888.

37. Nietzsche, *Beyond Good and Evil*, 68, §56.

38. Nietzsche, *Beyond Good and Evil*, 53, §43. These words are put in the mouth of the "philosopher[s] of the future," the "coming philosophers." The following aphorism indicates the direct identification of these figures with Nietzsche himself.

39. See for example Nietzsche, fragments 24 [4], winter 1883–1884; 25 [1], spring 1884; 25 [323], spring 1884.

40. Nietzsche, fragment 24 [4], winter 1883–1884, *Unpublished Fragments from the Period of* Thus Spoke Zarathustra *(Spring 1884–Winter 1884/85)*, 585.

41. Nietzsche, "Why I Am a Destiny," *Ecce Homo*, 333, §8. Trans. mod. It should not escape us that this phrase, "breaking humanity in two," was used close to two millennia earlier by certain Gnostics (particularly Basilides) to describe . . . Christ.

42. Nietzsche, "What I Owe to the Ancients," *Twilight of the Idols*, 91, §5.

43. Nietzsche, "What I Owe to the Ancients," *Twilight of the Idols*, 91, §5.

44. Nietzsche, fragment 5 [1], 1, autumn 1882: "Will to live? I have always only found will to power in its place." *Unpublished Fragments from the Period of* Thus Spoke Zarathustra *(Spring 1884–Winter 1884/85)*, 166.

45. See Nietzsche, "On Old and New Tablets," *Zarathustra*, III, §3; "Why I Am So Clever," *Ecce Homo*, §10.

46. Nietzsche, fragment 25 [7], December 1888–January 1998.

47. Nietzsche, "On Old and New Tablets," *Zarathustra*, III, 163, §12.

48. See Hans Jonas, "Gnosticism and Modern Nihilism," *Social Research* 19 (December 1952), as well as Eric Voegelin, *Science, Politics, and Gnosticism* (Wilmington, DE: ISI Books, 2004 [1958]).

49. Nietzsche, *The Anti-Christ*, in *The Anti-Christ, Ecce Homo, Twilight of the Idols, and Other Writings*, trans. Judith Norman (Cambridge: Cambridge University Press, 2005), 66.

29. This etymology is indeed viable, with *eurus* meaning "vast" or "open" and *ôps* meaning "gaze" or "view." Herodotus, however, says that the origin of the name is unknown (*Histories* 4.45). There are, of course, many "Europes"—and different ones for Hesiod, Homer, Pindar, etc.

30. Nietzsche, "The Wanderer and His Shadow," §275: "The democratization of Europe is irresistible" (*Human, All Too Human*, 376).

31. Nietzsche, "The Wanderer and His Shadow," 215. On this point, see Ernst Troeltsch, *Der Historismus und seine Probleme* (Tübingen: Mohr, 1922), chaps. III/2 and III/3.

32. Nietzsche, "The Wanderer and His Shadow," §215, *Human, All Too Human*, 365.

33. Nietzsche, "Assorted Opinions and Maxims," §171, *Human, All Too Human*, 252.

34. Nietzsche, *The Gay Science*, 158, §103.

35. Nietzsche, "Assorted Opinions and Maxims," §171, *Human, All Too Human*, 253.

36. Nietzsche, "Assorted Opinions and Maxims," *Human, All Too Human*, 323.

37. Nietzsche, *Human, All Too Human*, 174, §475.

38. Nietzsche, "The Wanderer and His Shadow," §87, *Human, All Too Human*, 332. See the end of aphorism 246 of *Beyond Good and Evil* where Nietzsche compares two prose writers who "were confounded": the one who distills his words like cold drops from "the ceiling of a damp cave" (Parsifal's!)—that is, Wagner—and one who fights with a "flexible rapier"—that is, Nietzsche himself (or possibly Lessing, whom Nietzsche always admired for his style) (*Beyond Good and Evil*, 183).

39. Nietzsche, *Beyond Good and Evil*, 177, §242.

40. See Nietzsche, fragments 9 [142], 11 [2], 16 [10], 1887.

41. Nietzsche, *Human, All Too Human*, §285.

42. Nietzsche, *The Gay Science*, §329.

43. *The Gay Science*, 108, §42. Trans. mod.

44. Nietzsche, *On The Genealogy of Morals*, III, §25.

45. Nietzsche, *Beyond Good and Evil*, 175, §241.

46. Nietzsche, *Beyond Good and Evil*, 227, §287.

47. Nietzsche, *Human, All Too Human*, 175, §475. It is plausible that the free spirit will be able to maintain the necessary tension between the philosopher and the artist which coexist in conflict within him. But it is by no means certain that the overman, who appears in *Zarathustra*, does not represent a "prophetic" tension of fusion and overcoming. Nietzsche, in claiming this, would be going against the very idea of the eternal return (cf. *Beyond Good and Evil*, §43) and would succumb to the temptation of a conception of genius that opens a new era—while in fact this would merely be a regression toward the influence of Schopenhauer and Romanticism.

48. Nietzsche, *Human, All Too Human*, 175, §475.

49. Heinrich von Treitschke, "Unsere Ansichten," translated as "The Jews Are Our Misfortune" in Richard S. Levy, *Antisemitism in the Modern World: An Anthology of Texts* (Lexington, MA: D. C. Heath, 1991), 70.

50. Treitschke, "Unsere Ansichten," 70.

51. W. Boehlich, *Der Berliner Antisemitismusstreit* (Frankfurt am Main, 1965), 242.

52. Nietzsche, *Beyond Good and Evil*, 187, §251.

53. Nietzsche, *Beyond Good and Evil*, 187, §251.

54. Nietzsche, *Beyond Good and Evil*, 188.

55. Nietzsche, *Beyond Good and Evil*, 188. Walter Kaufmann adds the following footnote: "Something made; something born; something fictitious and unreal."

56. Nietzsche, *Beyond Good and Evil*, 188.

57. Nietzsche, *Beyond Good and Evil*, 189.

58. Epictetus, *Enchiridion*, trans. George Long (Mineola, NY: Dover, 2004), chap. 33, 14. Cf. Jean Paul's formula, "The art of silence is one of the many arts of speech," which Nietzsche quotes in fragment 29 [142], summer–autumn 1877 (Nietzsche praises Jean Paul in opposition to Fichte in aphorism 244 of *Beyond Good and Evil*).

59. Nietzsche, *Beyond Good and Evil*, 189, §252.

60. Nietzsche, *Human, All Too Human*, 132–33, §285.

61. Nietzsche, *Beyond Good and Evil*, 191, §253.

62. Nietzsche had read *Madame Bovary* . . .

63. Nietzsche, *Beyond Good and Evil*, §255.

64. Nietzsche, *Beyond Good and Evil*, 197, §256.

"The Purest Race in Europe . . ."

1. Nietzsche calls Paul "the greatest of all apostles of revenge" (Nietzsche, *The Anti-Christ*, 45, 44). See also the end of aphorism 42: "*What* was the only thing that Mohammed would later borrow from Christianity? Paul's invention, his method of priestly tyranny, of forming of herds, the belief in immortality—*which is to say the doctrine of 'judgment'* . . ." (*The Anti-Christ*, 42, 39).

2. Nietzsche, "The Wanderer and His Shadow," §85, *Human, All Too Human*, 332.

3. See Nietzsche, fragment 3 [137], 201, spring 1880.

4. This is the term Domenico Losurdo uses in his monumental work *Nietzsche, il ribelle aristocratico* (Turin: Bollati Boringhieri, 2000). In English: *Nietzsche, the Aristocratic Rebel*, trans. Gregor Benton (Chicago: Haymarket Books, 2021).

5. See Nietzsche, fragments 26 [374] and 26 [432], summer–autumn 1884, among other passages, as we have seen previously. Nietzsche, *Unpublished Fragments from the Period of* Thus Spoke Zarathustra *(Spring 1884–Winter 1884/85)*, 230 and 246.

6. See Arthur Schopenhauer, *The World as Will and Representation*, book 3, chap. 48, where he refers to "a small, isolated, capricious, hierarchical (i.e., ruled by false notions), obscure people, like the Jews, despised by the great contemporary nations of the East and of the West" (trans. E. F. J. Payne, vol. 1 (New York: Dover, 1969), 232).

7. Nietzsche to Richard Wagner, May 22, 1869. The Nietzsche Channel.

8. Nietzsche, "Nietzsche's Library," compiled by Rainer J. Hanshe. Nietzsche Circle, 2007, 21. http://www.Nietzschecircle.com/. Gersdorff had called

Wagner's 1969 work *Das Judenthum in der Musik* illuminating. Nietzsche takes up the patristic and scholastic use of the term "Jewish," meant to designate an attachment to the empirical and the literal. The "day when men shall be noble" is a quotation from memory (and incorrect) of Goethe's epilogue to Schiller's *Song of the Bell* (Goethe had spoken of a day "for the noble being").

9. Nietzsche to Siegfried Lipiner, August 24, 1877. The Nietzsche Channel.

10. Wagner, "Public and Popularity," in Richard Wagner, *Religion and Art*, trans. William Ashton Ellis (Lincoln: University of Nebraska Press, 1994), 57.

11. Catherine Alison Phillips, *Cosima Wagner* (New York: Knopf, 1931), 742.

12. Here is the text of that letter:

Herewith I am returning to you the three issues of *Correspondenz* [a well-known anti-Semitic journal], thanking you for permitting me to cast a glance at the muddle of principles that lie at the heart of this strange movement. Yet I ask you in the future not to provide me with these mailings: I fear, in the end, for my patience. Believe me: this abominable "wanting to have a say" of noisy dilettantes about the *value* of people and races, this subjection to "authorities" who are utterly rejected with cold contempt by every sensible mind (e.g., E. Dühring, R. Wagner, Ebrard, Wahrmund, P. de Lagarde—who among these in questions of morality and history is the most unqualified, the most unjust?), these constant, absurd falsifications and rationalizations of vague concepts, "Germanic," "Semitic," "Aryan," "Christian," "German"—all of that could in the long run cause me to lose my temper and bring me out of the ironic benevolence with which I have hitherto observed the virtuous velleities and pharisaisms of modern Germans.—And finally, how do you think I feel when the *name Zarathustra* is mouthed by anti-Semites? . . .

Nietzsche to Theodor Fritsch, March 29, 1887, The Nietzsche Channel, trans. mod.

13. Bernhard Förster, a high school professor, was responsible for the first large-scale anti-Semitic movement in the new Reich. On April 13, 1881, on his initiative, 267,000 signatures were collected and sent to Bismarck in a petition to restrict Jewish immigration, to exclude Jews from all spheres of decision-making and general education, as well as demanding their enrollment in a "register." Förster upheld the ideas that Jesus was an Aryan, that Jews were responsible for all societal ills, and that the German spirit was contaminated by Jewish literature and music. From 1879 on, he continued to send Nietzsche anti-Semitic propaganda (*Antisemitische Correspondenz*), where Nietzsche could observe, with indignation, that his work was referenced. In 1882 Förster was dismissed as a teacher, after publicly assaulting people he believed to be Jewish in the street. See, on the theme of Jesus as an Aryan, Maurice Olender, *The Languages of Paradise: Race, Religion, and Philology in the Nineteenth Century*, trans. Arthur Goldhammer (Cambridge: Harvard University Press, 2009), 69–71, 95–105.

14. See fragment 32 [32], start of 1874–spring 1874: "The danger is great for Wagner if he does not give any value to Brahms, etc. or to the Jews."

15. Nietzsche declared this to be true himself; see *Beyond Good and Evil*, §251; fragments 12 [116] and 15 [43], autumn 1881: "Germans today fall into two categories: Jews and anti-Jews."

16. Nietzsche, *Human, All Too Human*, 175, §475.

17. Nietzsche, *Human, All Too Human*, 175, §475.

18. Nietzsche, *Human, All Too Human*, 175, §475.

19. Nietzsche, *Human, All Too Human*, 174, §473, 174.

20. Nietzsche, *Human, All Too Human*, 175, §475.

21. Nietzsche, "Why I Am So Clever," *Ecce Homo*, 240, §2.

22. Nietzsche, *Dawn*, 150, §205.

23. Nietzsche, *Dawn*, 150, §205.

24. Nietzsche, *Dawn*, 152.

25. Nietzsche, *Dawn*, 152.

26. Cf. Leo Strauss, "Why We Remain Jews" (1962), who says of this aphorism: "This is the most profound and most radical statement on assimilation which I have read." Leo Strauss, *Jewish Philosophy and the Crisis of Modernity*, ed. Kenneth Hart Green (Albany: SUNY Press, 1997), 325. It goes without saying for Strauss that the establishment of a State of Israel goes against Nietzsche's vision, even though, as we know, Strauss considered this State to be one among other aspects of exile (in the sense of *Galut*).

27. Nietzsche, *The Gay Science*, 291, §348. In aphorism 361, he says that "the Jew" is "the true master of the European press" (*The Gay Science*, 317).

28. Nietzsche, *Dawn*, 152, §205.

29. Nietzsche, *The Gay Science*, §348.

30. Nietzsche evokes the figure of Moses Mendelssohn only once (calling him the "archangel of pedantry"). He mentions the philologist Bernays only once, in a letter to Rhode of December 7, 1872, to underline the audacity of Bernays's claim that *The Birth of Tragedy* contained all his own theses, and to add that young Jewish philologists were "as always, at the forefront" of the field. Nietzsche was unaware of Reform Judaism as well as Judaic Studies founded by Leopold Zunz (1794–1886). Nor is he interested in the virulent reactions provoked by the strain within German Judaism personified by Rabbi Samson Hirsch. Everything he learned about the history of Judaism came through the Göttingen school (Julius Wellhausen in particular), thus by way of a rationalist and critical reading (calling itself "philological"), responsible for the very controversial classification of scriptural sources (Jahwist, Elohist, Sacerdotal, etc.), which remained a source of conflict until the 1950s, in the work of Gerhard von Rad for example.

31. See Nietzsche, fragment 8 [13], summer 1883: "Yes, the philosophy of law! This is a science which, like all moral sciences, is not even in diapers yet! [. . .] as long as jurisprudence fails to establish itself on new ground, namely in history and comparative studies of peoples, it will remain trapped in dreary battles between thoroughly false abstractions." *Unpublished Fragments from the Period of* Thus Spoke Zarathustra *(Summer 1882–Winter 1883/1884)*, 297, trans. mod. This fragment is nearly exactly reproduced two years later, in August–September 1885 (fragment 42 [8]). The first fragment dates from the end of the composition of *Zarathustra*; the second, from the writing of *Beyond Good and Evil*. These are the only two occurrences of the term *Rechtswissenschaft* in Nietzsche's work.

32. Nietzsche, *Dawn*, §84.

33. Nietzsche, *Beyond Good and Evil*, §52.

34. Nietzsche, *The Gay Science*, §99. See also aphorisms 135 and 141.

35. Nietzsche, fragment 3 [103], spring 1880.

36. Nietzsche, *Beyond Good and Evil*, 108, §195.

37. Nietzsche, *The Gay Science*, 309, §357. Here Nietzsche also writes: "(the

Jews become mawkish when they moralize)." The parenthetical comments on a reference to Philipp Mailänder, author of *Die Philosophie der Erlösung* (Berlin: Hofmann, 1879) . . . who was not, in fact, Jewish.

38. Nietzsche, "Morality as Anti-Nature," *Twilight of the Idols*, 29, §6.

39. This is Jaspers's position, despite the considerable care with which he reads Nietzsche.

40. Nietzsche, *The Gay Science*, 190, §141.

41. Nietzsche, *On the Genealogy of Morals*, III, §9.

42. Nietzsche, "On Truth and Lie in an Extra-Moral Sense," trans. Walter Kaufmann, in *The Portable Nietzsche*, ed. Walter Kaufmann (New York: Random House, 1980), 41.

43. Nietzsche, fragments 11 [148], 11 [157], 11 [202], 11 [205], autumn 1881.

44. See the chapter "The 'Will to Power': A Concept," above.

45. Cf. fragment 15 [66], autumn 1881: "Judaism [. . .] created an abyss between us and the Greeks"; and on Socrates, *Ecce Homo*, "Why I Write Such Good Books," "The Birth of Tragedy," §1.

46. Nietzsche, *Beyond Good and Evil*, 185, §250.

47. Nietzsche, *Beyond Good and Evil*, 185, §250. Trans. mod.

48. Nietzsche, *The Anti-Christ*, 21, §24.

49. Nietzsche, *Beyond Good and Evil*, 184, §248.

50. Nietzsche, *Beyond Good and Evil*, 186–87, §251.

51. Nietzsche, *Beyond Good and Evil*, 187. Trans. mod.

52. Nietzsche, *Beyond Good and Evil*, 188.

53. Nietzsche, *Beyond Good and Evil*, 188–89.

54. Nietzsche, *Beyond Good and Evil*, 189.

55. Nietzsche, *Beyond Good and Evil*, 189.

56. Nietzsche, *The Gay Science*, §109.

57. Nietzsche, *Beyond Good and Evil*, 161, §230. Trans. mod.

58. Nietzsche, *On the Genealogy of Morals*, 106, III, §7: "There also exists a peculiar philosophers' prejudice and affection in favor of the whole ascetic ideal; one should not overlook that."

59. Nietzsche, *Beyond Good and Evil*, 65, §51.

60. Nietzsche, *On the Genealogy of Morals*, 107, III, §7. Kaufmann provides the following translation: "Let the world perish, but let there be philosophy, the philosopher, *me!*"

61. Nietzsche, *On the Genealogy of Morals*, 33, I, §7.

62. Nietzsche, *The Anti-Christ*, 22, §25.

63. Nietzsche, *The Anti-Christ*, 21, §24.

64. Nietzsche, *Beyond Good and Evil*, §§9 and 13; *The Gay Science*, §4.

65. Nietzsche, *On the Genealogy of Morals*, 33–34, I, §7.

66. Nietzsche, *The Anti-Christ*, 23, §26.

67. Nietzsche, *The Anti-Christ*, 23, §26.

The Concept of "Race"

1. Alfred Rosenberg, *Der Mythus des 20. Jahrhunderts* (Munich: Hohenei-chen, 1930), 530.

2. Rosenberg, *Der Mythus des 20. Jahrhunderts*, 530.

3. Heinrich Härtle, *Nietzsche und der Nationalsozialismus* (Munich: Eher, 1937). Härtle was the successor of Bäumler at the Amt Rosenberg, the stronghold of Nazi propaganda. Convicted in 1945, he was released from prison in 1948 and pursued a career as a journalist and essayist in the West German far right, taking on the role of persistent and respected spokesperson for the movement (he died in 1986). Although other Nazis, such as Curt von Westernhagen and Christian Steding, reproached Nietzsche for his critique of anti-Semites and his anti-Germanism and anti-nationalism, there was never any real unanimity concerning Nietzsche among the ideologues at the center of the party, particularly on the question of "race." This assessment is important to remember. The idea of the supposedly inherent tendency of each "race" to develop by expansion, for the Nazis, was justified by the very principle of conservation that Nietzsche rejected, as we have seen. Moreover, all the racist conceptions clearly share the same substantialist premise: that "race" manifests by means of heredity through perceptible empirical characteristics indissociable from cultural and spiritual orientations that can be evaluated on the basis of the criterion established by Aryan superiority. Nietzsche rejects the idea that "races" exist whose purity ought to be preserved because they are supposedly "foundational" and would suffer from the mixture of blood: "NB. Against Aryan and Semitic. Where races are mixed, the source of great culture." Nietzsche, fragment 1 [153], autumn 1885–spring 1886, *Unpublished Fragments (Spring 1885–Spring 1886)*, 293.

4. Arno Schickedanz, *Das Judentum—eine Gegenrasse* (Leipzig: Weicher, 1927).

5. Härtle, *Nietzsche und der Nationalsozialismus*, 64.

6. See above.

7. Nietzsche, *Beyond Good and Evil*, 184–85, §248.

8. See Nietzsche, fragment 11 [124], spring–autumn 1881: "Some drives, such as the sex drive, are capable of great refinement, of a sublimation by the intellect [. . .]. As soon as a drive becomes intellectual, it takes on a new name and a new allure [. . .]. It often becomes *opposed* to the drive it was previously, just as its contradiction [. . .] continues its direct action at the same time."

9. Johann Gottlieb Fichte, "Berliner Vorlesungen über die Bestimmung des Gelehrten" (1811), *Werke*, vol. 11 (Berlin: De Gruyter, 1971), 192.

10. Furthermore, like all Gnostics, Fichte rejects the idea of "God the creator," viewing this figure as a bad demiurge, in favor of a God of light. Nietzsche, meanwhile, rails against both Marcionite Catholicism and, of course, Christianity, not without a biting irony: "A loving God becomes Jewish" (fragment 10 [55], autumn 1887). Beginning with the first of the *Untimely Meditations*, Nietzsche constantly flings mockery at Fichte's nationalist assertion that "True philosophy [. . .], which takes as its starting point the singular, pure divine life [. . .] is in fact simply German, that is, original" (Fichte, *Address to the German Nation*, *Werke*, 7: 362). Nietzsche, on the other hand, writes: "What bothersome heaviness, lassitude, dampness, bathrobes, how much 'beer' there is in German intelligence! [. . .] You can count the number of German men of knowledge who have ever had 'spirit' on two hands" (fragment 10 [7], autumn 1887).

11. Nietzsche, *Beyond Good and Evil*, 117–18, §203.

12. Nietzsche, *Unpublished Fragments from the period of* Human, All Too Human I *(Winter 1874/75–Winter 1877/78)*, 274.

13. Nietzsche, *Human, All Too Human*, 32, I, §36.

14. Nietzsche, *Human, All Too Human*, 12, I, §1.

15. In his acceptance of "physiology" Nietzsche is incontestably influenced by his reading of Darwin.

16. Nietzsche, *Dawn*, §435; *Beyond Good and Evil*, §15, and "Raids of an Untimely Man," *Twilight of the Idols*, §47. Fragment 11 [128], spring–autumn 1881: "Physiological movements take place through the activity of our human affects. The affects (struggle, etc.) are nothing other than interpretations of the intellect."

17. Nietzsche, *Human, All Too Human*, 36–37, I, §45. Trans. mod.

18. Nietzsche, fragment 10 [59], autumn 1887.

19. Nietzsche, fragment 11 [273], autumn 1881. Nietzsche speaks here of "Slavic-German-Nordic culture," calling it "inferior, but stronger and more hardworking."

20. Nietzsche, fragment 7 [306], end of 1880.

21. Nietzsche, fragment 21 [2], summer 1882.

22. Nietzsche, *The Gay Science*, 340, §377.

23. Nietzsche, fragment 11 [122], spring–autumn 1881: "The conflict of these drives is as necessary as any struggle: for suffering matters as little for the species as the destruction of countless individuals."

24. Nietzsche, *On the Genealogy of Morals*, 45, I, §13.

25. Nietzsche, *Dawn*, 180–81, §272.

26. It is nonetheless important to pay attention to this exception in section 5 of the first essay of *On the Genealogy of Morals*, where, in a parenthesis, "race" in Europe is discussed in the following manner: "the suppressed race has gradually recovered the upper hand again, in [hair] coloring, shortness of skull, perhaps even in the intellectual and social instincts: who can say whether modern democracy, even more modern anarchism and especially that inclination for '*commune*,' for the most primitive form of society, which is now shared by all the socialists of Europe, does not signify in the main a tremendous *counterattack*—and that the conqueror and *master race*, the Aryan, is not succumbing physiologically, too?" Nietzsche, *On the Genealogy of Morals*, 30–31. The "Aryans" he refers to are both Goths and Celts. The arresting aspect here is the relation established between a physiological atavism and a configuration of drives proper to the "oppressed": generally, for Nietzsche, atavism is deprived of any "material" basis, since the form of the body depends upon the determination of the values that compose it. Let us recall that when Nietzsche was writing *On the Genealogy of Morals*, he made this note (Nietzsche, fragment 5 [52], summer 1886–autumn 1887): "Maxim: avoid all people who participate in mendacious racial trickery."

27. [It should be noted that this is an anti-Black racist idea that persists to this day and is imbricated with the systemic denial of medical care to Black people, particularly in the United States, rendering them more vulnerable to premature death. For a nuanced historical reflection on this, see Christina Sharpe, *In the Wake* (Durham: Duke University Press, 2016).—Translator]

28. Nietzsche, *On the Genealogy of Morals*, 68, II, §7.

29. Nietzsche, *The Gay Science*, §42.

30. Nietzsche, fragment 14 [14], spring 1888.

31. Nietzsche, fragment 11 [273], autumn 1881.

32. Nietzsche, "Assorted Opinions and Maxims," *Human, All Too Human*, §223. Here the "method" is that of the critical historian as well as direct observa-

tion, including that of comparative ethnology: "to understand history we have to go in quest of the living remnants of historical epochs—we have to *travel*, as the father of history, Herodotus, travelled, to other nations—for these are only earlier *stages of culture* grown firm upon which we can *take a stand*" (*Human, All Too Human*, 268). See also fragment 23 [43], end of 1876–summer 1877: "in the end, the national state still wants a 'national' culture, thereby bringing the lack of clarity to its peak—for national and culture are contradictions. Even in the universities, the fortresses of science, there are people who, with the secretiveness of traitors, acknowledge religion and metaphysics as still-higher powers *above* science." *Unpublished Fragments from the Period of* Human, All Too Human I *(Winter 1874/75–Winter 1877/78)*, 381.

33. Nietzsche, fragment 26 [432], summer–autumn 1884. *Unpublished Fragments from the Period of* Thus Spoke Zarathustra *(Spring 1884–Winter 1884/85)*, 246.

34. Nietzsche, fragment 26 [432], summer–autumn 1884. *Unpublished Fragments from the Period of* Thus Spoke Zarathustra *(Spring 1884–Winter 1884/85)*, 246.

35. Nietzsche, fragment 27 [27], summer–autumn 1884. *Unpublished Fragments from the Period of* Thus Spoke Zarathustra *(Spring 1884–Winter 1884/85)*, 262.

36. Nietzsche, fragment 27 [29], summer–autumn 1884. *Unpublished Fragments from the Period of* Thus Spoke Zarathustra *(Spring 1884–Winter 1884/85)*, 262. Cf. fragment 10 [138], autumn 1887: "The same quantum of energy means different things at different stages of development. [. . .] The fact that the world does *not* move toward a stable state is the only thing that is *proven*. Consequently, we *must* understand its highest state as not being a state of equilibrium."

37. Nietzsche, fragment 25 [1], December 1888–start of January 1889.

In Fine

1. Nietzsche, fragment 26 [407], summer–autumn 1884. *Unpublished Fragments from the Period of* Thus Spoke Zarathustra *(Spring 1884–Winter 1884/85)*, 238–39.

Index